KHCPL Main

220 N. Union St.
Kokomo, IN 46901-4614
765.457.3242
www.KHCPL.org

| Obesity

Other Books of Related Interest:

> "Congress shall make no law . . . abridging the freedom of speech, or of the press."
>
> *First Amendment to the US Constitution*

The basic foundation of our democracy is the First Amendment guarantee of freedom of expression. The Opposing Viewpoints series is dedicated to the concept of this basic freedom and the idea that it is more important to practice it than to enshrine it.

I Obesity

Sylvia Engdahl, Book Editor

GREENHAVEN PRESS
A part of Gale, Cengage Learning

GALE
CENGAGE Learning·

Farmington Hills, Mich • San Francisco • New York • Waterville, Maine
Meriden, Conn • Mason, Ohio • Chicago

Elizabeth Des Chenes, *Director, Content Strategy*
Douglas Dentino, *Manager, New Product*

Articles in Greenhaven Press anthologies are often edited for length to meet page requirements. In addition, original titles of these works are changed to clearly present the main thesis and to explicitly indicate the author's opinion. Every effort is made to ensure that Greenhaven Press accurately reflects the original intent of the authors. Every effort has been made to trace the owners of copyrighted material.

Cover Image copyright © CLIPAREA I Custom media/Shutterstock.com.

LIBRARY OF CONGRESS CATALOGING-IN-PUBLICATION DATA

Obesity / Sylvia Engdahl, book editor.
    pages cm -- (Opposing viewpoints)
    Summary: "Opposing Viewpoints: Obesity: Opposing Viewpoints is the leading source for libraries and classrooms in need of current-issue materials. The viewpoints are selected from a wide range of highly respected sources and publications"-- Provided by publisher.
    Includes bibliographical references and index.
    ISBN 978-0-7377-7278-4 (hardback) -- ISBN 978-0-7377-7279-1 (paperback)
    1. Obesity. I. Engdahl, Sylvia, editor.
    RC628.O222 2014
    616.3'98--dc23
                                                                2014018240

Printed in the United States of America
1 2 3 4 5 6 7 18 17 16 15 14

Contents

Chapter 3: Should Society Actively Combat Obesity?

Chapter 4: What Is Causing the Rise in Obesity?

Why Consider
Opposing Viewpoints?

> *"The only way in which a human being can make some approach to knowing the whole of a subject is by hearing what can be said about it by persons of every variety of opinion and studying all modes in which it can be looked at by every character of mind. No wise man ever acquired his wisdom in any mode but this."*
>
> *John Stuart Mill*

In our media-intensive culture it is not difficult to find differing opinions. Thousands of newspapers and magazines and dozens of radio and television talk shows resound with differing points of view. The difficulty lies in deciding which opinion to agree with and which "experts" seem the most credible. The more inundated we become with differing opinions and claims, the more essential it is to hone critical reading and thinking skills to evaluate these ideas. Opposing Viewpoints books address this problem directly by presenting stimulating debates that can be used to enhance and teach these skills. The varied opinions contained in each book examine many different aspects of a single issue. While examining these conveniently edited opposing views, readers can develop critical thinking skills such as the ability to compare and contrast authors' credibility, facts, argumentation styles, use of persuasive techniques, and other stylistic tools. In short, the Opposing Viewpoints Series is an ideal way to attain the higher-level thinking and reading skills so essential in a culture of diverse and contradictory opinions.

In addition to providing a tool for critical thinking, Opposing Viewpoints books challenge readers to question their own strongly held opinions and assumptions. Most people form their opinions on the basis of upbringing, peer pressure, and personal, cultural, or professional bias. By reading carefully balanced opposing views, readers must directly confront new ideas as well as the opinions of those with whom they disagree. This is not to argue simplistically that everyone who reads opposing views will—or should—change his or her opinion. Instead, the series enhances readers' understanding of their own views by encouraging confrontation with opposing ideas. Careful examination of others' views can lead to the readers' understanding of the logical inconsistencies in their own opinions, perspective on why they hold an opinion, and the consideration of the possibility that their opinion requires further evaluation.

Evaluating Other Opinions

To ensure that this type of examination occurs, Opposing Viewpoints books present all types of opinions. Prominent spokespeople on different sides of each issue as well as well-known professionals from many disciplines challenge the reader. An additional goal of the series is to provide a forum for other, less known, or even unpopular viewpoints. The opinion of an ordinary person who has had to make the decision to cut off life support from a terminally ill relative, for example, may be just as valuable and provide just as much insight as a medical ethicist's professional opinion. The editors have two additional purposes in including these less known views. One, the editors encourage readers to respect others' opinions—even when not enhanced by professional credibility. It is only by reading or listening to and objectively evaluating others' ideas that one can determine whether they are worthy of consideration. Two, the inclusion of such viewpoints encourages the important critical thinking skill of objectively evaluating an author's credentials and bias. This evaluation will illuminate an author's reasons for taking a particular stance on an issue and will aid in readers' evaluation of the author's ideas.

It is our hope that these books will give readers a deeper understanding of the issues debated and an appreciation of the complexity of even seemingly simple issues when good and honest people disagree. This awareness is particularly important in a democratic society such as ours in which people enter into public debate to determine the common good. Those with whom one disagrees should not be regarded as enemies but rather as people whose views deserve careful examination and may shed light on one's own.

Thomas Jefferson once said that "difference of opinion leads to inquiry, and inquiry to truth." Jefferson, a broadly educated man, argued that "if a nation expects to be ignorant and free . . . it expects what never was and never will be." As individuals and as a nation, it is imperative that we consider the opinions of others and examine them with skill and discernment. The Opposing Viewpoints series is intended to help readers achieve this goal.

David L. Bender and Bruno Leone,
Founders

Introduction

"False and scientifically unsupported beliefs about obesity are pervasive in both scientific literature and the popular press."

—*"Myths, Presumptions, and Facts About Obesity,"*
New England Journal of Medicine,
January 31, 2013

Much has been said about the increase in the obesity rate during the past few decades, and it is often called an epidemic. While the extent of the increase has been challenged on the grounds that the definition of "obesity" has been changed and that statistics are now more accurate than in the past, there is no doubt that a large percentage of the population now weighs more than what medical authorities consider "normal."

At present, there is considerable controversy over the question of whether obesity is a disease rather than merely a risk factor for other diseases. In June of 2013, the American Medical Association (AMA) classified obesity as a disease. However, only about 60 percent of the members voted for that classification; the other 40 percent voted against declaring it a disease, and the committee that studied the issue had recommended against doing so as well.

Although it is widely believed that obese people are unhealthy, this is not always true. The majority of doctors consider obesity in itself unhealthy, but other experts disagree. Up to a third of obese people are "metabolically healthy obese" (MHO), meaning they do not have any signs of risk for diabetes or heart disease. Some experts think that since obese individuals may develop such signs in the future, they should not be called "healthy." However, as obesity specialists S. Heshka and D.B. Allison wrote in the October 2001 issue of the *International Journal of Obesity*, "We cannot foretell who will develop an obesity-related health problem. In fact, some persons who meet the criteria for obesity will live long lives free of any of the morbidities known to be influenced by obesity."

One of the most prevalent beliefs about obesity is that it causes type 2 diabetes and heart disease, as statistics show a clear association between obesity and these diseases. Yet a basic principle of science is that statistical association does not indicate anything about causation, and some researchers suspect that obesity may be an early symptom of diabetes rather than its cause. Scientists are careful to use the wording "associated with" rather than "causes," but the media—and many doctors—rarely make the distinction.

Though it is often assumed that most obese people could achieve lasting weight loss if they ate less and moved more, experts agree that this is not always the case. Studies have shown that dieting and exercise do not work permanently for most individuals; the weight lost through these measures is regained after a short time because the body's metabolism has been altered. As yet, science has not found a way to overcome this, but researchers are working toward that goal.

Whether everyone who weighs more than the amount arbitrarily defined as "normal" ought to lose weight is a controversial issue. Doctors who believe fat in itself is harmful say they should. On the other hand, it has been found that for some people, weight loss, especially repeated weight loss—known as "yo-yo" dieting—may do more physical harm than being obese. Paul Campos and his colleagues in the February 2006 issue of the *International Journal of Epidemiology* explain that "diet drugs, weight loss surgery, eating disordered behaviour, fad diets, and the chronic weight cycling they induce have serious side effects, up to and including death." Furthermore, activists in the size acceptance movement and their supporters believe that diversity is good and that there is nothing wrong with being overweight if a person is otherwise healthy.

It is generally thought by the general public that the word "fat" is derogatory and that it is more polite to say "overweight." Some people do use "fat" as an insult, usually in a context that would be insulting no matter what word they used, and therefore many individuals dislike it. However, size acceptance advocates, such as members of the National Association to Advance Fat Acceptance (NAAFA) and similar organizations, prefer the word "fat" because it is a descriptive term such as "thin," "tall," or "short." They find "overweight" objectionable because it implies that there is some particular weight standard to which everyone ought to conform. Furthermore, "fat" is a more general term because technically both "overweight" and "obese" have arbitrary medical definitions. In this book, all three terms are used, often interchangeably.

In today's society, prejudice against obese individuals seems to be widespread, and unlike prejudice against other groups, it is not yet considered unacceptable. Many think that using derogatory terms to insult individuals will motivate them to lose weight; however, studies have shown this increases the risk of becoming or staying obese. This may be because stress is a known cause of weight gain, and being the subject of discrimination and ridicule is extremely stressful and damages health.

The more science learns about obesity, the more apparent it becomes that its growing prevalence is a complicated issue that involves far more than the number of calories people eat and how much exercise they get. According to Cornell University sociologist Jeffery Sobal, "Obesity is a complex, dynamic, and multidimensional biosocial phenomenon, a synergistic product of the interaction between physiology and the social world."

The authors of the viewpoints in *Opposing Viewpoints: Obesity* explore the issue in chapters titled "Is There an Obesity Epidemic?," "Is Obesity a Disease?," "Should Society Actively Combat Obesity?," and "What Is Causing the Rise in Obesity?" The information presented in this volume provides insight into the perceived obesity epidemic, what is causing it, and what can be done to remedy it in today's society.

OPPOSING
VIEWPOINTS®
SERIES

CHAPTER 1

Is There an Obesity Epidemic?

Chapter Preface

The question of whether the rise in obesity should be termed an "epidemic" is controversial, but whatever one chooses to call it, the influence of the media on public perception of the situation cannot be denied. Many people believe that it has been blown out of proportion by news stories, sensational articles, and even the wording of scientific papers. Whether or not this is true, in order to evaluate information about obesity, individuals need to be aware of how the media normally deal with medical issues.

Media presentations focus on maximizing impact on the intended audience, and negative stories have greater impact than positive ones—referring to something as a crisis gets readers' attention. News writers, therefore, focus on the negative aspect of facts even if they do not mean to exaggerate them. This is particularly true of articles about obesity because it is a subject with widespread relevance about which people have strong feelings. As University of Chicago political science professor J. Eric Oliver wrote in his book *Fat Politics: The Real Story Behind America's Obesity Epidemic*, "Although the media often sensationalize and oversimplify complicated issues in order to attract public interest, in the case of obesity this has been taken to great lengths."

Additionally, statistics concerning medical risks are generally stated in a way that most individuals find misleading. As has often been pointed out by critics, it is customary to report relative risks rather than absolute risks. It means little to say that obesity doubles the risk of developing a particular disease without stating the percentage of risk for non-obese people, which in most cases is very small, so that it remains small even when doubled. Yet the health problems to which obesity can lead have been presented in a way suggesting that it involves not merely an increased risk of future illness, but the near certainty of it.

In a March 2008 article in *Sociological Forum* reporting on a study that compared scientific papers on obesity with media coverage, University of California, Los Angeles (UCLA) sociologists Abigail C. Saguy and Rene Almeling wrote: "We found some evidence that news media have 'thrown fat in the fire,' enframing the issue of obesity, while simultaneously highlighting individual blame for weight. Compared to the science on which they were reporting, the news media used more evocative metaphors and language to discuss this putative crisis."

They found that scientists themselves also intensified public reaction to obesity studies, writing up their research with journalists in mind and framing it with press releases and interviews. Saguy and Almeling commented, "A reward structure in which, all things being equal, alarmist studies are more likely to be covered in the media may make scientists even more prone to presenting their findings in the most dramatic light possible."

In addition to these uncalculated forms of media distortion, there are all too frequent cases of purposeful attempts to rouse emotions. Media want to attract audiences. Research is often funded by organizations—both commercial and nonprofit—hoping to advance their own point of view. According to Patrick Basham and John Luik, writing about obesity in the February 2, 2008, issue of the *British Medical Journal*, "Some in the public health community believe that deliberate exaggeration or, indeed, misrepresentation of the risks of diseases or certain behaviours or our capacity to prevent or treat them on a population-wide basis is justified, if not demanded, in the interests of health."

"Since many of the exaggerations come from people who understand the scientific uncertainties around overweight and obesity," Basham and Luik continue, "it seems that these individuals have adopted such an approach to the obesity epidemic. The unwelcome implications of this for science policy and for evidence-based medicine dwarf those of any obesity epidemic, real or imagined."

All of this is not to say that the increase in obesity does not present problems to society. However, it does mean that media presentation may heighten the degree of concern about it. The viewpoints in this chapter present conflicting opinions about the prevalence of obesity.

VIEWPOINT 1

"With health care costs already on the rise as America ages, the country's growing waistlines will present one of the future's most dire economic challenges."

The Obesity Epidemic Is America's Greatest Ongoing Crisis

Dan Carroll

In the following viewpoint, Dan Carroll argues that the rise in the percentage of people who are obese is a crisis for America not only because obesity is unhealthy, but even more worrisome, because of its economic impact. In his opinion, the obesity epidemic will lead to large increases in the health care costs borne by society and will cause a significant decrease in the amount of money available for other needs, such as education. He believes the economy will be seriously damaged unless something is done to combat the obesity epidemic. Carroll is a writer for the Motley Fool, a financial services company.

As you read, consider the following questions:

1. According to the CDC, how many Americans were obese as of 2010?

2. Why, in Carroll's opinion, will the increase in obesity cause health care costs to rise, even for people who are not obese?

3. According to Carroll, why will the rise in obesity increase the cost of transportation?

In the year 2000, no U.S. state had an obesity rate above 30%. In 2010, 12 states did.

That's hardly the most shocking statistic of the obesity epidemic, America's most serious ongoing crisis. Much has been made about the health implications of being overweight: Between increased risks of diabetes to hypertension and other ailments, obesity brings a whole host of unwanted factors to sufferers. However, the worst consequence of this growing challenge isn't the health dilemma; it's the economic predicament sparked by rising obesity rates.

With health care costs already on the rise as America ages, the country's growing waistlines will present one of the future's most dire economic challenges—unless Americans get a handle on stopping the obesity outbreak today.

How Obesity Will Hurt Average Americans

35.7% of Americans were obese as of 2010, according to the CDC [Centers for Disease Control and Prevention]. The last two decades have seen a dramatic rise in its incidence, and the costs to overweight individuals have skyrocketed.

Health care spending alone for overweight Americans averaged more than $1,400 per year above what normal citizens paid, according to a 2006 study. The impact was even greater for obese individuals, who anted up more than $2,700 above the average American's health care spending. That amounted to obese people spending more than 5.5% more of their average household income in 2006 in health care spending as compared to normal-weight citizens.

Translate that to the waning fortunes of the average American's wallet, and it's easy to see how individuals are suffering financially under the weight of obesity. Rising costs of health insurance aren't helping: The health care reform laws of 2010 allow employers to charge obese employees up to 30% or higher for insurance if said employees opt out of wellness programs. However, the costs of health care reform won't impact the overweight alone.

Health insurers can't turn away customers with preexisting conditions any more, and insurance premiums could be ready to skyrocket. The CEO [chief executive officer] of Aetna, the third-largest health insurer in the U.S., predicted that unsubsidized premiums could rise between 20% to 50% on average under Obamacare [officially known as the Patient Protection and Affordable Care Act, a federal health care reform law passed in 2010]. Add up the rising health care costs of obesity onto what insurers will have to pay out, and now *everyone's* hurting. Pooled insurance may actually help obese customers manage costs, while hindering healthy and normal-weight individuals who will pay more to subsidize the group.

This all comes as more and more Americans struggle to deal with stagnant wages and high unemployment. Obesity alone has contributed to those factors: Studies show correlation between chronic obesity and unemployment.

Rising health care costs due to obesity won't just cripple individuals' financial flexibility in coming years; they will deliver a crushing blow to the U.S. economy and businesses in the long term.

What the Crisis Means to the Economy

Here's another statistic indicative of the problem the country's facing: Obesity-related health care spending is estimated to cost up to $190 billion per year; or more than 20% of total U.S. health care costs. If nothing's done to stop the epidemic now, chalk up an additional $50 billion or more on top of that total by 2030.

Obesity's rising costs are *not* what the U.S. economy needs as the government attempts to put a lid on exploding health care expenditures. The U.S. spent more than $8,000 per person on health care in 2012, or more than 17% of GDP [gross domestic product]—more than 2.5 times the OECD [Organisation for Economic Co-operation and Development] average for national health care spending per person, a trend that fits as the U.S. has the highest obesity rate of any OECD nation.

That's money that can't be spent on other vital areas of the economy, such as education, transportation, or even budget balancing—critical necessities the nation will have to address in coming years. If health care spending continues to grow, however, those will have to be put on the back burner. And grow it has: While the rate of health care spending growth has fallen by around 50% from 2003 to 2012, this growth still outpaces overall economic growth. The fall may only be temporary, as obesity—along with the aging of the Baby Boomers—strains the health care system.

Speaking of transportation, that too will take a critical hit from obesity's rise. Studies estimate that increased passenger weight contributed to an extra $275 million in airline fuel costs between 1990 and 2000 alone. Airlines can't afford that in today's perilous industry climate; Southwest Airlines, for instance, can charge obese passengers for an extra seat. Yet that may not be enough for Southwest and other carriers if obesity and high fuel costs continue to weigh on their bottom lines; Southwest only manages a 2.5% profit margin, hardly allowing much breathing room.

Businesses will see even more costs due to obesity if rates keep climbing. Studies have shown correlation between workplace absenteeism and obesity, and more overweight Americans will hamper firms' productivity. Estimates peg absenteeism-related losses for American businesses at up to $6 billion or more per year, according to data from a Duke University study led by Eric Finkelstein.

Signs of Hope in the Crisis

While many businesses—and the economy at large—will be hurt by the unabated rise of obesity, some stand to gain.

Health care companies offer hope for American businesses. Medical device manufacturers—in particular, companies with major orthopedics branches such as Johnson & Johnson and Stryker—stand to gain with rising obesity rates. More overweight Americans mean more customers who need hip- and joint-servicing products to manage higher weight loads, and Johnson & Johnson and Stryker rank among the top companies in those departments.

Expect pharmaceutical firms entrenched in the diabetes market to thrive as well. Obesity-related diabetes has surged across the U.S., with the CDC estimating that 8.3% of the population—or more than 25 million people—suffered from the disease in 2010. Diabetes alone inflicted $174 billion in total estimated costs in 2007, and firms have profited off the disease's rise: Merck's Januvia and Janumet family of diabetes medications pulled in more than $5.7 billion in sales in 2012. Competitors like Johnson & Johnson are pushing into the diabetes market as well, keen to make a buck off America's growing problem.

Companies will capitalize regardless of what happens, but it's not too late for America to beat back the obesity epidemic before it capsizes the economy. A 5% reduction in BMI [body mass index] in every U.S. state could reduce health care spending by 7% or more, freeing up billions of dollars for the many needs of the future. Smaller waistlines would mean less fuel expenditure for airlines, cars, and other means of transportation, cutting down on both costs and emissions.

How can America start fighting back against obesity? Media campaigns always help, and the "Let's Move!" campaign from First Lady Michelle Obama has sparked public awareness about the problem. Still, more is needed, and the answer could come from how the country pushed back against the health hazards of smoking. Media campaigns, advertising regulations, and taxation helped *drive* back tobacco's toll, all while mostly avoiding dreaded public health–influenced bans that can often hurt as much or more than they help—as New York's ban on large soft drinks (and going way back in time, Prohibition) has shown.

Whether it's by taxing high-calorie or high-fat foods or incentivizing fitness and lower body fat percentage rates through ongoing health care reform actions, more impacting action is needed to confront the challenges of obesity. If nothing is done to combat this epidemic, America's greatest crisis will only grow larger—threatening the financial security and freedom of individual Americans, businesses, and the future of the economy as a whole.

It's time for America to step up and drive back obesity's costly advance. The well-being of the future demands nothing less.

"Two studies produced by the US Centers for Disease Control and Prevention (CDC) ... completely undermine the claims of an obesity epidemic."

The Myth of an "Obesity Tsunami"

Patrick Basham and John Luik

In the following viewpoint, Patrick Basham and John Luik report on the results of published obesity studies conducted in both America and England. The figures the studies present show no significant increase in obesity for most categories of children and adults, and only a small increase in boys with the highest weight. The authors conclude that the government is unwisely attempting to cure a nonexistent disease. Basham is the director of the Democracy Institute and an adjunct scholar at the Cato Institute. Luik is a senior fellow at the Democracy Institute. They are coauthors, with Gio Gori, of Diet Nation: Exposing the Obesity Crusade.

As you read, consider the following questions:

1. According to published information from the National Health and Nutrition Examination Survey, how much increase in adult obesity was there between 1999 and 2008?

2. What change in the prevalence of childhood obesity was found by the Health Survey for England?

3. According to the viewpoint, what common belief besides the existence of an obesity epidemic is contradicted by the results of the studies mentioned?

Everyone knows the truth about obesity: We're getting fatter each year. Our growing girth is termed everything from the "pandemic of the twenty-first century" to an "obesity tsunami". But the evidence is now flooding in from both America and England that obesity is the epidemic that never was.

Two studies produced by the US Centers for Disease Control and Prevention (CDC) and published last week [in January 2010] in the *Journal of the American Medical Association*— one about obesity in children and adolescents, and the other about adult obesity—completely undermine the claims of an obesity epidemic.

Both studies are based on information from the National Health and Nutrition Examination Survey from 2007–08, which is a representative sample of the American population. The survey measured the heights and weights of 3,281 children and adolescents and 219 infants and toddlers, as well as 5,555 adult women and men. The study of children and adolescents looked at the body mass index (BMI) of children and adolescents over five time periods between 1999 and 2008, the decade during which child obesity was widely described as America's preeminent public health problem.

The Language of War

Announcing a public health crisis and evoking an epidemic has historically lent a sense of urgency that can—like declaring war—justify abridging civil liberties (think quarantine). Indeed, the framing of fat as an impending health disaster has been used as justification for the "war on obesity." This "war on obesity" has unfolded simultaneously with the "war on terror" and has mirrored it in interesting ways. . . .

The language of war creates fear, making citizens easier to manipulate and more willing to give up civil liberties. The "war on terror" metaphor was used to gain wartime powers for former president George W. Bush. . . . The "war on obesity" metaphor has been used, among other things, to shift federal funding from tobacco research to obesity research and from food stamps to obesity prevention, to speed up Food and Drug Administration (FDA) approval of weight-loss drugs and overlook potential side effects, and to send "BMI [body mass index] report cards" home to parents in Arkansas and Pennsylvania. In extreme cases, the war on obesity has been used to justify removing fat children from their parents' custody. On an individual level, the "war on obesity" language sets people up to regard their own body fat with hostility, as they fight their personal "battles of the bulge."

Abigail C. Saguy, What's Wrong with Fat?
New York: Oxford University Press, 2013.

The results are striking. During none of the five periods was there a statistically significant trend, except for boys at the highest BMI levels. In other words, if there was a spike in obesity, it was confined to a very small number of very obese boys.

What about the adult "couch potato" generation? Here, again, the results put the lie to claims of an obesity tsunami. In the study of adults, the researchers also looked at obesity trends over the past decade. For women, there were no statistically significant changes in obesity prevalence over the entire decade, while for men there were no prevalence differences during the last five years of the decade. As the researchers note, obesity prevalence may have "entered another period of relative stability".

A similar absence of an obesity epidemic is to be found in England. According to the Health Survey for England, which collected data from 7,500 children and almost 7,000 adults, there has been a decline in the prevalence of overweight and obesity for adult men, while for adult women prevalence has remained the same.

Comparing the results of the survey for 2007 with those of 2004, there have been either declines or no significant changes in male prevalence of overweight and obesity in all age groups from 16–54. As for children, the survey finds: "There was no significant change in mean BMI overweight/obesity prevalence between 2006 and 2007, and there are indications that the trend in obesity prevalence may have begun to flatten out over the last two to three years."

For example, there was a decrease in obesity in girls aged two to 15 years old between 2005 and 2006, from 18 per cent in 2005 to 15 per cent in 2006. Among boys aged two to 10 years old, the prevalence of overweight declined from 16 per cent in 2005 to 12 per cent in 2006. According to the results, overweight and obesity have been declining amongst boys and girls aged two to 15 since 2004. In girls, obesity prevalence levels are largely unchanged from where they were in 2001.

The findings of the English survey not only contradict the claim that we are in the midst of an obesity epidemic, but they also debunk the public health establishment's erroneous claim that increases in children's weight are due to junk food advertising and too many sugary soda drinks. According to the survey, the root cause of any weight gains that one does see appear to lie in physical activity levels. For example, "21 per cent of girls aged two to 15 in the low physical activity group were classed as obese compared with 15 per cent of the high group".

A similar pattern was found in the 2006 survey, which found that 33 per cent of girls aged two to 15 with low levels of physical activity were either overweight or obese compared with 27 per cent of those with high levels of physical activity. As with smoking, obesity prevalence was higher in both boys and girls in the lowest income group.

Clearly, governments' current course of draconian regulatory treatment seeks to cure an illusory disease. The nanny state's infatuation with an obesity epidemic that does not exist is a searing indictment of this particular public health crusade.

> "BMI [body mass index] significantly underestimates prevalence of obesity when compared to . . . direct measurement of percent body fat."

The Prevalence of Obesity Has Been Underestimated

Nirav R. Shah and Eric R. Braverman

In the following viewpoint, Nirav R. Shah and Eric R. Braverman discuss a study they conducted of how obesity is measured, and they conclude that more people are obese than statistics show. They explain that body mass index (BMI), which compares a person's height and weight, is not a good way to measure fat. They describe a more accurate method that they believe gives a better estimate of a person's risk of developing obesity-related diseases. Shah, a physician, is the commissioner of health for New York State. Braverman is the founder and president of PATH Foundation NY, a medical research organization.

As you read, consider the following questions:

1. Why is body mass index (BMI) used to determine obesity even though it is known to be an imprecise way to measure body fat?

Nirav R. Shah and Eric R. Braverman, "Measuring Adiposity in Patients: The Utility of Body Mass Index (BMI), Percent Body Fat, and Leptin," *PLoS One*, April 2, 2012. Licensed under CC by 3.0. Reproduced by permission.

2. According to Shah and Braverman, what factors of obesity are not taken into account when it is defined by BMI?

3. What percentage of men and women did Shah and Braverman find to be misclassified as obese or non-obese when diagnosed by means of their BMI?

Global trends of increasing obesity threaten public health and contribute to the burden of disease as much as smoking does. Obesity is associated with increased risk of diabetes, hypertension, heart disease, stroke, cancer, dyslipidemia [abnormal amount of fat in the blood], liver and gallbladder disease, sleep apnea and respiratory problems, osteoarthritis, abnormal menses and infertility. Adiposity in midlife strongly relates to reduced probability of healthy long-term survival in women. Obesity has become a priority of national, state and local public health efforts and in the care of individual patients. Thus, clinical detection of obese individuals has commensurately reached critical importance.

With the increasing importance of obesity detection, it is useful to reevaluate how body fat is determined. For adults, the body mass index (BMI) is commonly used. Its popularity stems in part from its convenience, safety, and minimal cost, and its use is widespread, despite not being able to distinguish lean body mass from fat mass. The United States Centers for Disease Control and Prevention (CDC) explain: "For adults, overweight and obesity ranges are determined by using weight and height to calculate a number called the 'body mass index' (BMI). BMI is used because, for most people, it correlates with the amount of body fat." However, the BMI is actually an indirect surrogate measurement considered imprecise.

Recent estimates from NHANES [National Health and Nutrition Examination Survey], a nationally representative health examination survey, project that approximately 34% of adult Americans are overweight (defined as a BMI between

25–30 kg/m^2) and an additional 34% are obese (BMI >30 kg/m^2). In contrast, the CDC estimates rates of obesity over 20% in all 50 states with estimated rates over 30% in 12 states. These estimates are fundamental to US policy addressing the epidemic of obesity and are central to designing interventions aimed at curbing its growth, yet they may be flawed because they are based on the BMI.

The outdated BMI formula [BMI = weight in pounds/ (height in inches)^2 x 703], developed nearly 200 years ago by [Adolphe] Quetelet, is not a measurement of adiposity, but merely an imprecise mathematical estimate. Defining obesity based on percent body fat, as with BMI, also has arbitrary cut-points. In 1995, the World Health Organization (WHO) defined obesity based on a percent body fat ≥25% for men and ≥35% for women, while the most recent 2009 guidelines from the American Society of Bariatric Physicians (ASBP), an American Medical Association (AMA) specialty board, used percent body fat ≥25% for men and ≥30% for women. The ASBP percent body fat guidelines identify individuals that are suitable candidates for treatment for obesity with anorectic agents [medications that causes loss of appetite]. Most studies comparing BMI with more accurate measures of adiposity used cutoffs of body fat >25% for men and >30% for women.

BMI ignores several important factors affecting adiposity. Greater loss of muscle mass leading to sarcopenic obesity [increased proportion of body fat due to loss of muscle mass] in women occurs increasingly with age. BMI does not acknowledge this factor, exacerbating misclassifications. Furthermore, men's BMI also does not consider the inverse relationship between muscular strength and mortality. It fails to take into account that men lose less muscle with age than women. . . .

A Different Way to Measure

We sought to characterize the degree of misclassification of obesity based on BMI using percent body fat from DXA [dual-

Percentage of Body Fat and BMI for All Patients

		Men N=518	Women N=875	Total N=1393
Concordant	BMI non-obese, % body fat non-obese	265 (51%)	227 (26%)	492 (35%)
	BMI obese, % body fat obese	122 (24%)	225 (26%)	347 (25%)
Discordant	BMI non-obese, % body fat obese	116 (22%)	423 (48%)	539 (39%)
	BMI obese, % body fat non-obese	15 (3%)	0 (0%)	15 (1%)

TAKEN FROM: Nirav R. Shah and Eric R. Braverman, "Measuring Adiposity in Patients: The Utility of Body Mass Index (BMI), Percent Body Fat, and Leptin," *PLOS One*, April 2, 2012.

energy X-ray absorptiometry, a means of measuring bone density] in a large, unselected population, and to use the more accurate DXA-derived measure to identify the optimal cut-points for defining obesity using BMI. Reclassifying obesity cut-points is worth considering, as there is a population of in-dividuals with a normal BMI who nonetheless have increased adiposity as determined by more sensitive methods; these are the so-called 'normal weight obese.' These individuals may have increased risk for medical comorbidities [simultaneous conditions] such as hyperlipidemia, coronary artery disease, hypertension, and diabetes. Furthermore, in the intermediate ranges, BMI is not a good discriminator of cardiovascular risk; use of adiposity measures rather than BMI may be a bet-ter predictor, but have recently failed. Therefore, there is a need to reclassify the obesity epidemic, identify clinically use-ful biomarkers, and clarify what the medical and scientific communities are measuring with BMI. . . .

The table [shown] demonstrates the discordance seen between classifications of obesity based on BMI versus percent body fat. While there was agreement for 60% of the sample, 39% were misclassified as non-obese based on BMI, while meeting obesity criteria based on percent body fat. Only 1% was classified as obese based on BMI, but non-obese by percent body fat. A total of 48% of women were misclassified as non-obese by BMI, but were found to be obese by percent body fat. In sharp contrast, 25% of men were misclassified as obese by BMI, but were in fact non-obese by percent body fat (i.e., the muscular body morphology). . . .

BMI significantly underestimates prevalence of obesity when compared to DXA direct measurement of percent body fat. Currently, no other blood test or biomarker has been correlated with the rate of obesity. The use of both DXA and leptin [a hormone involved in weight regulation] levels offers the opportunity for more precise characterization of adiposity and better management of obesity.

This misclassification was seen more commonly in women than in men and occurred more frequently with advancing age in women. A more appropriate cut-point for obesity with BMI is 24 for females and 28 for males. These new cut-points increased diagnostic sensitivity with small losses in specificity. Clinicians should consider using 24 as the BMI cut-point for obesity in women, in order to maximize diagnosis and prevention of obesity-related comorbidities. Public health policy makers should also consider these more accurate cut-points in designing interventions. The Healthy People 2010 goal was to reduce rates of obesity (defined using BMI >30) from 23% in 1988–1994 to the target of 15%. Not only was this goal unmet, but in light of this data we may be much further behind than we thought. Our results document the scope of the problem of false-negative BMIs, emphasize the greater misclassification in women of advancing age, and confirm the improved precision available by gender-specific revised cutoffs. . . .

How Should Obesity Be Determined?

A definitive recommendation regarding which patients need DXA requires further study. The ASBP is using both BMI and DXA as criteria for interventions, and this may be a reasonable transition in public health policy. Some may prefer to use DXA alone, though the cost-effectiveness of this strategy is questionable. Given sufficient volume, DXA scans with body fat and bone density may be conducted efficiently at low cost.

Since a recent study showed that the significant lowering of leptin impacts long-term weight control, the idea of utilizing leptin as a component in the national attack on obesity might be considered. To date, no other blood test or biomarker has correlated with the rate of obesity, while most of our other public health priorities have good biomarkers.... The use of both DXA and leptin levels offers the opportunity for more precise characterization of adiposity and perhaps management of obesity. In the future, by measuring leptin, an entirely new range of treatment options may eventuate....

NHANES estimates that 28.6% of adult American women are overweight (BMI 25–30 kg/m^2) and an additional 35.5% are obese (BMI >30 kg/m^2). Shifting those currently considered overweight into the obese category would clarify the magnitude of the issue of obesity. By our cutoffs, 64.1% or about 99.8 million American women are obese.

BMI significantly underestimates adiposity. A better cut-point for obesity with BMI is 24 for females and 28 for males. These body fat and leptin corrected BMI cut-points are consistent with lower cut-points for all-cause mortality in men and women. Leptin levels enhance the precision of estimation in using BMI. The findings can be generalized since this was a cross-sectional study of the American population. Obesity, body fat and increased adiposity are more prevalent than the American public and American physicians are aware of. This is contributing greatly to multiple comorbidities such as hyperlipidemia, coronary artery disease, hypertension, and diabetes. The current systematic underestimation of adiposity in large-scale studies, and subsequent use of such studies for public health policy making, can readily be corrected, resulting in a more appropriate sense of urgency and more cogent weighing of public health priorities. While BMI is less precise than direct adiposity measures in predicting medical comorbidities, improving this globally used metric will have broad population health implications.

> "One magical night in June of 1998 twenty-nine million Americans went to bed with average figures and woke up fat. . . . The task force had simply lowered obesity standards."

The Obesity Epidemic Was Manufactured by the Weight Loss Industry

Linda Bacon

In the following viewpoint, Linda Bacon argues that the belief that obesity is invariably harmful to health is promoted by the weight loss industry and that pharmaceutical companies put large amounts of money into research that exaggerates the risks of being overweight. She states that the majority of obesity researchers have financial ties to the industry and that the results of studies unfavorable to industry are often suppressed. Nevertheless, she feels that most individuals with conflicts of interest sincerely believe that obesity always leads to death and disease. Bacon is a nutrition professor at City College of San Francisco and the author of Health at Every Size: The Surprising Truth About Your Weight, *from which this viewpoint is excerpted.*

As you read, consider the following questions:

1. According to Bacon, who besides the weight loss industry benefits from exaggerated claims about negative health consequences of obesity?

2. On what grounds did prominent national magazines and others criticize an article in the *Journal of the American Medical Association* that attributed four hundred thousand deaths to overweight and obesity, forcing the journal to later print a correction?

3. According to Bacon, why do obesity researchers tend to accept cultural assumptions about negative effects of being fat?

It pays for the weight-loss industry to have us believe that weight has negative health consequences, as is evident from the enormous resources that the pharmaceutical industry has put behind research that exaggerates the health risks associated with weight. Knoll Pharmaceuticals, for example, offers funding to those who "advance the understanding of obesity as a major health problem," as they explicitly state in a call for proposals. After mobilizing concern about obesity, they can profit by selling the cure.

Exaggerated claims regarding the dangers of obesity are in fact at the cornerstone of efforts to get Food and Drug Administration [FDA] approval for long-term use of weight-loss drugs known to be hazardous. When defending themselves against lawsuits, the pharmaceutical companies justify sales with the argument that obesity is so dangerous that it overshadows the dangers of their drugs.

Exaggeration of obesity's dangers similarly benefits physicians, for whom there is a tremendous market in promoting various weight-loss methods, particularly surgery. It mobilizes patients to use their services—and helps secure insurance coverage. Health practitioners are among the most insidious players in this fat-hating drama, as they have legitimized the cultural mandate for thinness by reframing it as a health concern. Bariatric surgery poses a particularly egregious example. Ironically, as [political science professor J.] Eric Oliver astutely points out, bariatric surgeons actually *create* disease, by damaging a healthy organ, and justify this practice by asserting an imaginary disease, obesity.

Political Influence

The government has played a particularly potent role in propagating this cultural hysteria. It was unlikely a mere coincidence that the article wrongly attributing 400,000 deaths to overweight and obesity appeared in *JAMA* [*Journal of the American Medical Association*] just days before Julie Gerberding, the director of the CDC [Centers for Disease Control and Prevention], was to appear before Congress to request increased funding. The report was prepared not by the CDC's top experts on the subject but by Gerberding herself, who holds no particular expertise in obesity, and other researchers attached to her office. Gerberding, of course, cited the paper in her testimony.

The *Wall Street Journal* and *Science* magazine both noted that anonymous sources within the CDC were concerned that the report had been influenced by political pressure to make the results consistent with CDC's public health policy. The report was so blatantly problematic that even conventional obesity researchers questioned its methodology and conclusions, suggesting that a political agenda to exaggerate the risk of obesity had trumped scientific concerns. A host of reasons were expressed, among them that the authors added an arbitrary number of deaths from poor nutrition to the obesity category. The following *JAMA* issue featured several contentious letters. The criticism prompted an internal review and the CDC was eventually forced by a Freedom of Information Act request to post the results of this review on its Web site.

The updated information was eventually published in *JAMA* and . . . reduced the estimate for excess deaths a whopping 94 percent.

Lest people actually allow the data to inform practice, the CDC's next step was to issue a disclaimer to state health agencies stating that "despite the recent controversy in the media about how many deaths are related to obesity in the United States, the simple fact remains: obesity can be deadly." Apparently the CDC doesn't want the evidence to distract us from continuing to impose baseless policy.

Conflict of Interest

Also problematic is that those who determine public policy and federal-grant funding are almost always simultaneously on the payrolls of weight-loss and/or pharmaceutical companies, thus presenting a conflict of interest. Government panels favor economic interests over health interests whenever they identify obesity as a major public health threat, define obesity at low standards, promote unsuccessful treatments, or minimize the dangers of various treatments.

For instance, at least seven of the nine members on the National Institutes of Health's (NIH) obesity task force were directors of weight-loss clinics, and most had multiple financial relationships with private industry. Thanks to this task force, one magical night in June of 1998 twenty-nine million Americans went to bed with average figures and woke up fat. They woke up with a presumed increased risk of type 2 diabetes, hypertension, and atherosclerosis and a government prescription for weight loss. Of course, nobody gained a pound. The task force had simply lowered obesity standards, a change which was obviously favorable for private industry.

The research presented in their report did not support the value of lowering the standards. Indeed, the only relevant peer-reviewed research they cited in their report, a review of studies on the association between BMI [body mass index] and mortality, suggested that *raising* the standards would be a more astute application of the science. The review didn't find a statistically significant relationship between BMI and mortality until BMIs in excess of 40 (yet they set the cutoff for overweight at 25 and for obesity at 30)!

Over the years I've been privy to rumors of a lot of dirty secrets among obesity researchers. There are way too many stories circulating about research results being suppressed when they are unfavorable to industry, industry writing papers under the name of prominent academics, bogus numbers being reported by researchers and government agencies, "scientific organizations" that front for private industry. . . .

Knowing many of the players and the pressure many of us feel from our universities to make ourselves known and bring in grant money, and given my own personal experiences of being tempted by potential conflicts of interest, it doesn't take a leap of faith to believe those rumors are true. Indeed, evidence is accumulating, and many exposés have already been written.

Examine the key players in the two major organizations for obesity researchers, the Obesity Society and the American Obesity Association (which recently folded), and you will not find a single officeholder who does not have some financial tie to a pharmaceutical or weight-loss company. Indeed, I cannot think of one obesity researcher, other than myself and the government researchers that are prohibited from these relationships, with a policy of refusing industry money.

[J.] Eric Oliver calls this a "health-industrial complex," built on a "symbiotic relationship between health researchers, government bureaucrats, and drug companies," and he and health writer Thomas Moore describe the interlocking relationships. Drug companies sponsor the research that defines health issues and fund the researchers who sit on government panels; government agencies rely on researchers to provide the data to support their funding requests; and drug companies rely on health advisories issued by government agencies to promote and justify their products. Everyone benefits from reinforcing the same (fearmongering) message.

Unchallenged Assumptions

While the very nature of these relationships is problematic and true corruption exists to some extent, I also believe that it is unlikely many of the people promoting the obesity myths are acting consciously to mislead us, and I am not suggesting all of those holding conflicts of interest are dishonest or part of a conspiracy. Indeed, I believe that most are well intentioned. Rather, the myths about obesity are so much a part of our culture, and the penalty for questioning them so high, that assumptions are not even recognized, let alone challenged. Many obesity warmongers are sincere in their belief that fat leads to death and disease. And for those concerned about Americans' health, the "obesity epidemic" is a convenient, attention-getting way to highlight problems with nutrition or activity habits.

Indeed, my concern is that obesity researchers are highly vulnerable to accepting cultural assumptions—even more so than the general public—because their status, reputation, and livelihood are in large part determined by how well they promote the diet and pharmaceutical industries. Career opportunities are limited if they choose not to participate, resulting in little incentive to question the status quo. The result is that cultural bias plays a role in every aspect of research, including our underlying assumptions, what research we choose to undertake, what gets published, and how we interpret and report scientific data.

Public/private conflicts of interest, combined with the extraordinary financial clout of the weight-loss industry, is not conducive to being open-minded about new ideas or making sure important research gets conducted or reported, or that the best information directs public policy and gets out to the general public.

Fearmongering about weight is worth billions to the health care system, government agencies, scientists, and the media. And it ties in seamlessly with cultural values. The result is that weight myths have become unquestioned assumptions, so strongly a part of our cultural landscape that we regard them as self-evident.

Exaggerated Threat

Yes, Americans have been gaining weight, though the degree to which this is true has been blown out of proportion. No doubt our weight gain is symptomatic of changing environmental conditions, and our eating and activity habits are part of those conditions. There is, however, little evidence to suggest that the symptom—weight—is a problem in and of itself. The epidemic exists only because we have defined it to exist. The epidemic will vanish as soon as we stop pathologizing weight and relegating people into baseless and arbitrary categories like overweight and obese. While I am not arguing that we encourage weight gain in order to improve health or that body weight is irrelevant to health, it is clear that the threat posed by our weight and the benefits of weight loss have been misinterpreted and exaggerated. At both extremes—high and low—body weight adversely affects health. But the vast majority of Americans fall closer to the middle of the body fat bell curve, where weight is little more than a benign marker of an individual's genetic predisposition to carry it. . . .

Encouraging weight loss as our first line of defense or attack is just bad science. Weight loss is not effective for prolonging life or managing many diseases. Furthermore, we don't have effective methods for maintenance of weight loss, and health may worsen as people lose and regain weight repeatedly. Ironically, the admonition to lose weight may actually have contributed to the very diseases it is prescribed to cure.

Though a heavy weight may be the result of imprudent lifestyle habits or underlying disease in some individuals, there are also many large people who eat sensibly, exercise regularly, and have excellent health readings—and many thin people who don't. Regardless, a low weight—or healthy lifestyle habits—shouldn't be a requisite for respect.

Size is a sloppy and unscientific way to judge someone's health or character, and the social and medical imperative for a thin body is not only misguided, it has caused much damage. *"Normal weight" is neither normal (most people exceed it) nor ideal in terms of health.* All that can be determined by judging people based on their weight is one's own level of prejudice.

"When being overweight or obese tipped from a contagion to an epidemic in the female population, it became acceptable for men to put on extra pounds, too."

The Public's Acceptance of Higher Weight Is a Serious Problem

Neil Snyder

In the following viewpoint, Neil Snyder argues that being overweight is more acceptable today than in the past and that this change of attitude started among young women. He suggests that this was due to the influence of Oprah Winfrey, whom he believes made college women feel it was okay to be overweight. In his opinion, even what has been considered "normal weight" is too high, and health experts have failed to lower the standard because of political pressure from the overweight and obese population. Snyder is a professor emeritus at the University of Virginia. He writes a daily blog and is the author of numerous books.

Neil Snyder, "Oprah and the Obesity Epidemic," *American Thinker*, January 21, 2012. Copyright © 2012 by Neil Snyder. All rights reserved. Reproduced by permission.

As you read, consider the following questions:

1. Why does Snyder believe that Oprah Winfrey was responsible for altering the public's attitude toward weight?

2. According to Snyder, what masks the severity of America's weight problem?

3. What national problems does Snyder think will arise if the trend toward obesity is not reversed?

Data released last week [January 2012] by the Centers for Disease Control and Prevention (CDC) contains good news and bad news. The obesity rate in the U.S. has leveled off, but 35.7 percent of our adult population is obese. That's about 78,000,000 Americans.

When I was in college, there were obese people on campus at the University of Georgia where I went to school, but they were the exception. College women, in particular, were concerned about their figures, and you didn't see many overweight women on campus. That was in the late 1960s and early 1970s. Today, if you walk around any college campus, you'll find that women who are not overweight stand out. Something dramatic happened.

Using terminology that Malcolm Gladwell introduced in his book *The Tipping Point: How Little Things Can Make a Big Difference*, at some point being overweight morphed from a contagion to an epidemic. I don't know exactly when it occurred, but at the University of Virginia, I knew it had happened when women in my leadership classes routinely wanted to do projects on Oprah Winfrey. There is no question that Oprah influences lots of people—particularly young women—and the way she touches their lives is difficult for most men to understand.

I used to tell my students that women are bellwethers in our society. If their attitudes change, men's attitudes quickly follow. Oprah is a sort of cult hero because she seems to have it all. She's rich. You may not know this, but Oprah's net worth is more than a billion dollars. She runs her own company, and *The Oprah Winfrey Show* that ran from 1986 to 2011 was just one of the many programs and products it has produced. All of the women in my classes knew intimate details about Oprah's life because they watched *The Oprah Winfrey Show* every day at 4:00, and Oprah shared that information with her audience.

Scheduling classes for women in our school at 4:00 was difficult since so many of them wanted to relax with Oprah from 4:00 to 5:00. It was like an intimate coffee club, and Oprah was the head of the group. Her influence on my female students was enormous. I must have seen two dozen presentations on Oprah Winfrey over the years, and every time I saw one, the women in the presenting group commented on Oprah's "weight problem," but they didn't talk about it as a problem.

Oprah fluctuates between being overweight and obese because her weight goes up and down like a yo-yo. She shared her trials and tribulations in weight control with her audience/friends on a regular basis, and since her audience was predominantly women, she invited guests to appear on her show that could touch women's hearts. Women, particularly young women, are conscious of and sensitive to comments about their weight. Oprah and her guests made them feel good about themselves despite their growing "weight problem."

The Tipping Point

It was obvious that the young women in my classes were concerned about being accepted for who they are—excess weight and all. They saw those extra pounds as an important extension of them as human beings, not as a problem to be solved. That's why I think you can make a compelling argument that *The Oprah Winfrey Show* was the tipping point for the obesity problem among women, particularly young women—because Oprah made being fat okay for large numbers of them. Since women are bellwethers, when being overweight or obese tipped from a contagion to an epidemic in the female population, it became acceptable for men to put on extra pounds, too. I believe that Oprah made it "Cool to be Fat."

In the 1990s, the surgeon general of the United States, Dr. C. Everett Koop, made obesity a national issue. When he did, the fireworks began. Dr. Koop presented mountains of data showing that our obesity problem is huge. He even proved that what doctors call "normal weight" is too high. In other words, "normal weight" isn't normal.

When Dr. Koop launched his campaign, 50 percent of U.S. citizens were overweight, and 25 percent of them were obese using "normal weight" tables that we know were wrong. The medical community responded immediately by arguing that their patients who were on "diets" were struggling unsuccessfully to lose enough weight to get down to "normal weight" and that adjusting the weight tables to reflect more accurate information could send many of them into depression.

When the debate ended, they modified the "normal weight" tables slightly, but to this day they still mask the severity of our nation's weight problem. The overweight and obese population in our country has enough political muscle, or fat, to prevent health experts from doing what they know is right.

Political Pressure

If you watch television, read newspapers, or listen to the radio, you will be inundated with stories, commercials, public service announcements, and talk show discussions about our "obesity problem." What Dr. Koop couldn't achieve from his government position because of enormous political pressure to maintain the status quo, the powers that be are trying to accomplish by promoting healthy eating habits. They are attempting to move our society toward another tipping point—one that reverses the undesirable and unhealthy pattern. Will they succeed? Only time will tell, but leveling off is far from a reversal. Obesity among children is still on the rise, and as they grow older, our overweight and obesity problem could get worse.

A 2010 report on obesity in the United States prepared by the Trust for America's Health (TFAH) revealed results that are virtually identical to the CDC results that were released last week:

- Adult obesity rates increased in 28 states in the past year.

- More than two-thirds of states (38) have adult obesity rates above 25 percent.

- Ten out of the 11 states with the highest rates of obesity were in the South—with Mississippi weighing in with the highest rates for all adults (33.8 percent) for the sixth year in a row.

- Adult obesity rates for blacks topped 40 percent in nine states, 35 percent in 34 states, and 30 percent in 43 states and D.C.

- Rates of adult obesity for Latinos were above 35 percent in two states (North Dakota and Tennessee) and at 30 percent and above in 19 states.

- Ten of the 11 states with the highest rates of diabetes are in the South, as are the 10 states with the highest rates of hypertension.

- No state had rates of adult obesity above 35 percent for whites. Only one state—West Virginia—had an adult obesity rate for whites greater than 30 percent.

- The number of states where adult obesity rates exceed 30 percent doubled in the past year, from four to eight—Alabama, Arkansas, Kentucky, Louisiana, Mississippi, Oklahoma, Tennessee and West Virginia.

- Northeastern and Western states had the lowest adult obesity rates; Colorado remained the lowest at 19.1 percent.

According to Dr. Jeffrey Levi, executive director of TFAH, "Obesity is one of the biggest public health challenges the country has ever faced, and troubling disparities exist based on race, ethnicity, region, and income." He's right, and you don't need to read the report to know that we have a serious problem. All you have to do is go to the mall or the Golden Corral. More than a third of Americans can look in the mirror and see the problem.

In 2008, U.S. health care costs associated with obesity were $147 billion, but we face a multitude of other problems that are a direct result of obesity, including lower wages, fewer work hours, higher air travel costs, and more gasoline consumption. Cutting to the chase, overweight and obesity costs threaten to bankrupt this nation if we don't solve the problem.

| *"The good news is that already there is a growing awareness of how harmful our current prevailing perspective is about [the weight loss] issue."*

The Public's Obsession with Weight Loss and Thinness Is Harmful

Rick Kausman

In the following viewpoint, Rick Kausman argues that people to-day are in a situation comparable to the one portrayed in the movie The Matrix—*they do not realize that there is an alternative to the focus on weight and weight loss that characterizes today's world. In his opinion, the weight loss industry is aware that dieting is ineffective and that it results in collateral damage; the industry has camouflaged the evidence of this so effectively that health care professionals and governments have been taken in. This is harmful to the public, he says, but it will change as more and more people learn to focus on well-being rather than weight loss. Kausman is an Australian physician who specializes in healthy weight management. He is the author of the best-selling book* If Not Dieting, Then What?, *which won the Australian Food Writers Award for best nutrition writing.*

As you read, consider the following questions:

1. What main groups does Kausman say are keeping the public trapped by the beliefs about weight that he considers false?

2. According to Kausman, why do many health professionals support current assumptions about the relationship between weight and health?

3. What historical examples of false medical beliefs does Kausman consider comparable to today's belief that dieting is desirable?

I have always loved the movie *The Matrix*. I watched it again recently with my daughter Meaghan, and I can't help but be struck by the parallels of the situation that Neo, Morpheus and their allies find themselves in in the movie, with the circumstances of a growing number of people who are fighting passionately for a change in our culture.

If you have seen the movie, you will know that in *The Matrix*, the community is trapped in a world where there is no awareness that anything else outside their perceived world exists, even though there *is* a world outside. This lack of awareness is through no fault of the community inside the Matrix.

Similarly, in the world we live in (across many countries), through no fault of their own, a large number of the general community are unaware that there is a world that exists outside an all-consuming focus on weight and weight loss dieting. They are trapped in a real-life, weight-focused Matrix. Within this Matrix, communities have been sold the idea that the way to health and happiness is just a matter of finding the right diet, that it is simple and easy to achieve the weight of their dreams, and not only that, if weight is regained after a weight loss diet, then it is each individual's fault, not the result of a diet that was doomed to fail from the outset.

Another parallel in *The Matrix* is that, in the movie, there are fierce protectors of the Matrix. Their job is to make sure the minds of people in the Matrix are not awoken to the fact that there is something beyond the world within the Matrix. These protectors of the Matrix are there to defend it at all costs.

Similarly, in our world, we have protectors of our own weight-focused Matrix. I think we have two main groups protecting and/or creating barriers for millions of people trapped within the weight-focused Matrix. Firstly, those people who are aware that they are protecting the Matrix, namely, the 'commercial weight loss industry'; and secondly, those who I believe, are unwittingly protecting the Matrix, for example, many health professionals and governments.

The Commercial Weight Loss Industry

I have no doubt that most of the businesspeople involved in the commercial weight loss industry are aware of the ineffectiveness of the services and/or products they are selling. They are aware that weight loss dieting is ineffective, that weight loss dieting leads to weight regain for the majority of those who participate in it (therefore ensuring repeat business), and that weight loss dieting confers considerable collateral damage at many different levels.

A number of years ago I was asked to sit on a government committee of invited stakeholders to discuss what the government of Australia might be able to do to help with the so-called 'obesity crisis'. As it turned out, I was seated next to the CEOs [chief executive officers] of two major commercial weight loss companies. As we were waiting for the resumption of the day after the morning tea break at which muffins, fruit, tea and coffee were provided, I couldn't help but hear the discussion that was going on between the two CEOs. One said to the other as he was munching on an apple, "You know, I really felt like (eating) the muffin, but I thought (eating) the apple would look better."

To me, that simple sentence summed up the commercial weight loss industry beautifully—all show and no substance. But what should we really expect? The commercial weight loss industry is a business and it is self-serving. Their primary job is to make money for themselves and their shareholders. And as protectors of the weight-focused Matrix, so far anyway, they have done a very skillful job of creating the perception that they are part of the health community when nothing could be further from the truth. They have done an incredible job of camouflaging truth and evidence, and they have been brilliant at protecting their business, and by so doing, protecting the research evidence and the truth from the community, and thus protecting the weight-focused Matrix.

Health Professionals and the Government

As for the two groups that unwittingly protect the weight-focused Matrix, let's look at health professionals first. As incredible as it is, at best there is very limited and often no real training on the relationship between weight and health (at both undergraduate and postgraduate levels), in almost all, if not every, different health professional group (certainly in Australia). This includes, but is not only confined to, health professionals that many people consult with for advice *specifically* in this area of health such as doctors, dietitians, and psychologists. Due to this lack of training, there is very little understanding of this complex health issue. To fill the gap in training, it should be no surprise to any of us that the current weight-focused paradigm becomes the default position for many health professionals. And thus many health professionals continue to unwittingly protect the weight loss dieting, weight-focused Matrix.

Many governments have also become unwitting protectors of the weight-focused Matrix. Unfortunately their framework and understanding is often built from those who speak loudest (and from those who often have the most money to make a noise), and their effectiveness is most often limited to what is of benefit for *them* in short election cycles. From misguided so-called 'community service announcements' to full-blown media campaigns that have used a shaming approach in an attempt to create change (for example in the USA, 'Stop Sugarcoating It, Georgia' and in Australia, Western Australia, 'The Toxic Fat campaign'), governments have inadvertently and unwittingly continued to protect the weight-focused Matrix.

Can We Really Crack the Weight-Focused Matrix?

I think it is understandable to wonder if we could ever really crack the weight-focused Matrix. Could it really be possible for there to be no more weight loss commercial organisations selling their wares? Could it really be possible for us not to be bombarded with advertisements for meal replacements, quick-fix exercise equipment and quick-fix weight loss programs? Could it be possible for the present common cultural paradigm of weight being a matter of 'energy in, energy out' ever change?

I believe it must, it can, and it will. In not too long, I am confident that people will be looking back at this period of time in amazement. And they will be wondering how communities could have bought into the whole weight-focused paradigm for so long.

I believe in years to come, people will be reflecting back on this time and saying things like:

- How could we have thought that weight loss dieting could help people be healthy?

- How could health professionals become so obsessed with a person's weight that they lost sight of looking after the person?

Why Word Choice Matters

How do you refer to people at the heavier-than-average end of the weight bell curve? Currently, in mainstream U.S. society, the O-words, "overweight" and "obese," are considered more acceptable, even more polite, than the F-word, "fat." In the field of fat studies, there is agreement that the O-words are neither neutral nor benign. . . . In fat studies, there is respect for the political project of reclaiming the word *fat*, both as the preferred neutral adjective (i.e., short/tall, young/old, fat/thin) and also as a preferred term of political identity. There is nothing negative or rude in the word *fat* unless someone makes the effort to put it there; using the word *fat* as a descriptor (not a discriminator) can help dispel prejudice. Seemingly well-meaning euphemisms like "heavy," "plump," "husky," and so forth put a falsely positive spin on a negative view of fatness.

"Overweight" is inherently anti-fat. It implies an extreme goal: instead of a bell curve distribution of human weights, it calls for a lone, towering, unlikely bar graph with everyone occupying the same (thin) weights. If a word like "overweight" is acceptable and even preferable, then weight prejudice becomes accepted and preferred. . . .

Calling fat people "obese" medicalizes human diversity. Medicalizing diversity inspires a misplaced search for a "cure" for naturally occurring difference. Far from generating sympathy for fat people, medicalization of weight fuels anti-fat prejudice and discrimination in all areas of society.

Esther Rothblum and Sondra Solovay, eds.,
The Fat Studies Reader. *New York:*
New York University Press, 2009.

- How could the weight loss industry become so ubiqui-
tous for a number of decades when the evidence was
clear that its methods didn't help and were harmful for
so many?

And looking back at history, it is amazing how relatively
quickly things can change. Let me share with you two examples to highlight how things that are accepted as truth at
one time, can, in the future, be seen for what they really are.

The first example is from the early 1960s, when a brand of
sedative medications, promoted particularly for pregnant
women, was being marketed by the relevant pharmaceutical
company as being particularly safe. The medication was called
Distaval and the generic name: Thalidomide. [Thalidomide
contributed to thousands of babies being born with birth de-
fects.]

The second example I want to highlight was discussed in a
tremendous book entitled *The Heroic Client* by [Barry L.]
Duncan, [Scott D.] Miller and [Jacqueline A.] Sparks. The
story is about the 67-year-old former president of the United
States, George Washington. The story goes that on one particular day, Washington was out riding his horse and started
to feel unwell with a sore throat. On returning home from his
horse riding, his condition gradually worsened. The next day,
three doctors were called in to assess the situation. The physicians prescribed and delivered the best treatment of the day.
After a period of time, with no change in his condition, the
three doctors agreed that more of the same treatment was required. Unfortunately Washington deteriorated further and
despite two additional treatments, he died. What was this
treatment that was regarded as the best accepted panacea for
the time? Bloodletting.

I think these two examples highlight beautifully how things
at a certain time in history can appear to be the right thing to
do. However, with time and greater understanding, they would
be the last thing used to help or treat a certain condition.

Punching Holes in the Matrix

The good news is that already there is a growing awareness of how harmful our current prevailing perspective is about this issue, and how life is possible outside the weight-focused Matrix. We are just starting to gain some traction on many levels. And as momentum builds towards the inevitable shift away from a weight and weight loss dieting focus, we can all contribute to punching holes in the weight-focused Matrix in our own way, right now.

With every person with whom we share a comment, a thought, or a story that has a focus on well-being rather than weight loss, we punch another hole in the Matrix. With every positive media article, blog and tweet, we punch another hole in the Matrix. For every health professional who supports each and every patient or client they see with a focus on well-being rather than on weight loss, we punch another hole in the Matrix.

With every Health at Every Size and like-minded talk that is given to the general public, we punch multiple holes in the Matrix. With every Health at Every Size and like-minded training program delivered to health professionals, we punch multiple holes in the Matrix.

And with every government and workplace that starts to understand the short- and long-term benefits of taking a person-centred, well-being, Health at Every Size approach to health and health care delivery, we create more and more opportunities to punch holes in the Matrix.

Periodical and Internet Sources Bibliography

The following articles have been selected to supplement the diverse views presented in this chapter.

Paul Campos	"Our Absurd Fear of Fat," *New York Times*, January 2, 2013.
Laurie Cunningham	"Behold: The World's 10 Fattest Countries," GlobalPost, November 25, 2009.
David H. Freedman	"How Junk Food Can End Obesity," *Atlantic*, July–August 2013.
Kate Harding	"What Michelle Obama's Childhood Obesity Project Gets Wrong," *Salon*, February 10, 2010.
David L. Katz	"Is Obesity Cultural?," *U.S. News & World Report*, October 4, 2012.
Elizabeth Kolbert	"XXXL: Why Are We So Fat?," *New Yorker*, July 20, 2009.
Tina Moffat	"The 'Childhood Obesity Epidemic': Health Crisis or Social Construction?," *Medical Anthropology Quarterly*, vol. 24, no. 1, March 2010.
Abigail C. Saguy and Rene Almeling	"Fat in the Fire? Science, the News Media, and the 'Obesity Epidemic,'" *Sociological Forum*, vol. 23, no. 1, March 2008.
Pieter H.M. van Baal et al.	"Lifetime Medical Costs of Obesity: Prevention No Cure for Increasing Health Expenditure," *PloS Medicine*, February 5, 2008.
White House Task Force on Childhood Obesity	"Solving the Problem of Childhood Obesity Within a Generation," May 2010.

OPPOSING
VIEWPOINTS®
SERIES

CHAPTER 2

Is Obesity a Disease?

Chapter Preface

In June of 2013, the American Medical Association (AMA) voted to classify obesity as a disease. This decision drew both praise and angry objections. Many experts believed the labeling of obesity as a disease to be an example of medicalization, the process of redefining ordinary human problems as illnesses requiring medical treatment. Both supporters and opponents of medicalization say that one of the main reasons for it is financial. Health insurance does not pay doctors for helping people with problems not officially defined as diseases. Furthermore, it is difficult to get funding for medical research on conditions not considered diseases.

Opponents further believe that however sincere most doctors may be in their desire to help people, the driving force behind medicalization is the desire of treatment providers and pharmaceutical companies to cash in on normal aspects of being human. "There's a lot of money to be made from telling healthy people they are sick," wrote Ray Moynihan and his co-authors in a 2002 article in the *British Medical Journal*. "Some forms of medicalising ordinary life may now be better described as disease mongering: widening the boundaries of treatable illness in order to expand markets for those who sell and deliver treatments."

Disease mongering is a pejorative term defined by science writer Lynn Payer as "trying to convince essentially well people that they are sick, or slightly sick people that they are very ill." One way of doing this is to define conditions known to be risk factors for disease as diseases themselves. High blood pressure is an example; people who have it are not sick, but it increases their risk for heart attack and stroke; therefore, it has come to be viewed as an illness. The same thing has now happened in the case of obesity, which was formerly considered merely a risk factor for diabetes and other serious diseases. Both reclassifications involve immense profits for the pharmaceutical industry.

Another argument against medicalization is that it causes people who vary from the norm to feel defective and to be perceived that way by others. Some people find the labeling of obesity as a disease objectionable for this reason; they feel that it is degrading to call someone sick merely on the basis of his or her size. Many experts have described medicalization as a form of social control. Sociologist Peter Conrad in his book *The Medicalization of Society* writes, "This control is manifested in how medical expectations set the boundaries for behavior and well-being as well as how medical norms drive behavior." He goes on to point out, "When the cause [of behavior] is seen as biological and subject to 'medical excuse,' the individual is no longer considered responsible for the behavior."

Occasionally medicalization has been reversed: for instance, homosexuality, which was once considered pathological rather than a human variation, was removed from psychiatry's official manual of mental disorders in 1973. Healthy overweight people believe that viewing size variation as pathological is no different, and that classifying obesity as a disease is therefore a step backward. Whether obesity can justifiably be called a disease is likely to remain controversial. The viewpoints in this chapter explore the issue of obesity as a disease.

| *"Obesity is a very complex biological illness brought on by genetic, hormonal, neurochemical, environmental factors."*

Declaring That Obesity Is a Disease Will Help Patients

Mark J. Holland

In the following viewpoint, Mark J. Holland expresses his approval of the American Medical Association's recent decision to classify obesity as a disease. For too long, he says, obesity has been viewed as a mere lifestyle problem, in spite of extensive scientific evidence showing that it is a biological illness. Official recognition that obesity is a disease will, in his opinion, be of great help to patients and will focus attention on its prevalence, which he considers a public health disaster. Holland is a physician who specializes in medical treatment of obesity.

As you read, consider the following questions:

1. Why, in Holland's opinion, did the American Medical Association not classify obesity as a disease sooner?

2. What does Holland believe will be the most important result of classifying obesity as a disease?

3. What common attitude toward obesity does Holland say must change?

It's hard to believe that it took this long, but the American Medical Association (AMA) has finally voted to recognize obesity as a real disease. I'd like to spend a few minutes talking about why this recognition took so long and what it may mean in the years ahead for patients in the US who are obese.

The Stubborn Belief That Obesity Is Self-Inflicted

Perhaps the biggest reason it's taken the AMA so long to come around on the issue of obesity is (was) the view, held by many physicians, that obesity is simply a lifestyle problem resulting from poor food choices and inactivity. This view has persisted despite truly vast amounts of medical and scientific data showing that nothing could be further from the truth and that in fact obesity is a very complex biological illness brought on by genetic, hormonal, neurochemical, environmental factors. It is in fact, today, in the year 2013, crystal clear that obesity is a disease and not the result of some character flaw in its suffers.

So why do many doctors still believe otherwise?

In my honest opinion, the answer is simple prejudice. Doctors are people, and like all people they sometimes hold beliefs that are informed not by intellect or evidence but by emotion. Most doctors receive very little formal training in obesity, and lacking a basic professional understanding of the illness, they tend, like most people, to reflexively view the condition as caused by gluttony and sloth. Over the 23 years that I have practiced bariatric medicine, hardly a week passes when I don't hear yet another story from an obese patient about a doctor or other health care worker who treated them insensitively. Given how common this is, it's not surprising that it took the AMA so long to come around.

The AMA's Opinion About the Decision Was Not Unanimous

If obesity is to be considered a disease, a better measure of obesity than BMI [body mass index] is needed to diagnose individuals in clinical practice. Further research is also warranted into the physiologic mechanisms behind why some obese individuals (e.g., the metabolically healthy obese) do not develop adverse health outcomes related to excess adipose tissue. This is particularly relevant given the difficulties most people have in achieving sustained weight loss. In addition, much more research is needed to develop effective and affordable obesity prevention and management strategies at both the clinical and community levels.

Without a single, clear, authoritative, and widely accepted definition of disease, it is difficult to determine conclusively whether or not obesity is a medical disease state. Similarly, a sensitive and clinically practical diagnostic indicator of obesity remains elusive. Obesity, measured by BMI, is clearly associated with a number of adverse health outcomes, with greater consistency across populations at the highest BMI levels. However, given the existing limitations of BMI to diagnose obesity in clinical practice, it is unclear that recognizing obesity as a disease, as opposed to a "condition" or "disorder," will result in improved health outcomes. The disease label is likely to improve health outcomes for some individuals, but may worsen outcomes for others.

Report of the Council on Science and Public Health of the American Medical Association, June 2013.

What Will the AMA's Recognition Do to Help Obese Patients?

Regardless of why it's taken so long, the good news is that finally the AMA has acted and from that a number of positive changes are likely to emerge. Probably the most important change will come with health insurance. The AMA's recognition of obesity as a disease is going to put political pressure on insurance companies to finally begin reimbursing doctors for obesity care. At the moment, very few insurance companies do this, and most patients who seek care for their weight from doctors such as myself have to pay the full cost for their treatment out of pocket. It may take a while, but, thanks to the AMA announcement, this should start to change.

Also, the recognition of obesity as a disease is just the right thing to do. Today, sixty percent of the US population is overweight or obese, and rates of type 2 diabetes are skyrocketing around the nation. We have been in the middle of a full-blown obesity epidemic for more than a decade, and it's well past time that this public health disaster is given the recognition that it is due. It's also time for attitudes to change. Nobody (I hope) blames a person sick with, say cancer, for being ill, and nobody should ever thus blame a person sick from obesity. Obese people need compassion and help just like everyone else and, despite the delays, today's announcement by the AMA is a huge step in the right direction.

> "The AMA's move is actually a way for its members to receive more federal dollars, by getting obesity treatments covered under government health plans."

Obesity Is Not a Disease

Michael Tanner

In the following viewpoint, Michael Tanner argues that classifying obesity as a disease was a mistake because it will result in government meddling in a situation he believes is the result of individual behavior. Although obesity is a real problem, he says, it should not be dealt with by encouraging costly medical treatment for it. Moreover, he expects that shifting the responsibility for weight loss from obese individuals to society will lead to government regulation of the food industry. Tanner is a senior fellow at the Cato Institute, a public policy research organization.

As you read, consider the following questions:

1. According to Tanner, why will the classification of obesity as a disease require everyone to pay more for health care?

2. What kind of government interference in private affairs does Tanner expect will result from viewing obesity as a disease?

3. Why, according to Tanner, might calling obesity a disease make weight loss more difficult?

Recently the American Medical Association [AMA] declared that it will consider obesity a disease. At first glance, it's a minor story, hardly worth mentioning, but in reality the AMA's move is a symptom of a disease that is seriously troubling our society: the abdication of personal responsibility and an invitation to government meddling.

No one denies that this country faces a massive (no pun intended) obesity problem. The United States has one of the highest obesity rates in the world, with more than a third of all Americans believed to be obese and another third considered overweight. Obesity leads to a host of both long- and short-term health problems and costs Americans more than $190 billion annually in higher medical costs, and possibly as much as $450 billion in indirect costs, such as lost productivity.

But while obesity is a real problem, the AMA's move is actually a way for its members to receive more federal dollars, by getting obesity treatments covered under government health plans. A bipartisan group of congressmen has already seized on the AMA declaration as they push for Medicare coverage of diet drugs. Observers also expect an effort to expand Medicare reimbursement for bariatric surgery, aka stomach stapling. And there will almost certainly be pressure to mandate coverage for these things by private insurance carriers, under both state laws and the [Patient Protection and] Affordable Care Act.

Medicare and some private insurers already cover bariatric surgery for people who have a body mass index (BMI) of 35 or higher, making them morbidly obese, and who also have an obesity-related disease. Now there will be pressure to cover the procedure for those with much lower BMIs and those without related medical issues.

© Bob Englehart, "Fast Food Tax," PoliticalCartoons.com, 2010.

After the AMA decision, John Morton, treasurer of the American Society for Metabolic and Bariatric Surgery, was almost giddy, calling the AMA decision a "tipping point" and adding that "now coverage policy must catch up to that consensus." Since a typical bariatric surgery costs as much as $40,000, that could be interpreted as a warning for all of us to get out our wallets. In the end, we will be paying more, through either taxes or higher premiums.

At the same time, the AMA decision shifts responsibility for weight loss from the individual to society at large, while expanded Medicare and insurance coverage socialize the cost of treating obesity, thereby inviting all manner of government mischief. After all, if being fat is not our fault, the blame must lie with food companies, advertising, or other things that need to be regulated. And if you and I have to pay for the food and exercise choices of others, we should have a say in those choices.

Already, Harold Goldstein, executive director of the California Center for Public Health Advocacy, has cited the AMA declaration to boost his group's efforts to ban junk food and tax soft drinks. Certainly we can expect New York mayor Michael Bloomberg to cite the AMA resolution in support of his efforts to ban 16-ounce drinks and otherwise regulate our behavior. The nanny state can now claim medical backing.

No one wants to minimize the pain of those struggling with weight problems. But in the end, more government involvement is not the answer to those problems. Indeed, it could actually make weight loss more difficult because, as the AMA's Council on Science and Public Health warned before it was overruled by the AMA's full body, "'medicalizing' obesity could intensify patient and provider reliance on (presumably costly) pharmacological and surgical treatments to achieve a specific body weight" and could "detract from creative social solutions" to foster healthy behavior. As Elliot Berry, a nutrition expert at Hebrew University [of Jerusalem], notes, "There is no magic bullet—no medicine—for obesity. The way out of obesity is to eat less and better and to move your body."

> *"The scientific physiological data just doesn't support long-term 'healthy obesity' on a micro or macroscopic level. Fat cells are metabolically active and too many of them are eventually harmful."*

The AMA's Classification of Obesity as a Disease Is Proper

Sara Stein

In the following viewpoint, Sara Stein discusses the American Medical Association's (AMA's) classification of obesity as a disease, which she strongly favors. She is dismayed by the fact that many people have criticized the decision, including a committee of the AMA that recommended against it, and she offers responses to their arguments. In her opinion, scientific evidence shows that obesity is a disease in itself according to the usual definition of that term, and it is not just a risk factor for other diseases. Stein is a physician and psychiatrist. She is the author of Obese from the Heart: A Fat Psychiatrist Discloses *and the recipient of the 2010 Kaiser Permanente Ohio Humanitarian Award for Community Service.*

Sara Stein, "Why Obesity IS a Disease and How This New Definition Helps You Practice Medicine," American Holistic Medicine Association, July 2, 2013. Sara Stein, diplomate, American Board of Obesity; diplomate, American Board of Psychiatry and Neurology.

As you read, consider the following questions:

1. By what percentage did the American Medical Association pass its motion to classify obesity as a disease?

2. Why, in Stein's opinion, will obese people have health problems in the future even if they are presently healthy?

3. According to the American Medical Association, what are the criteria for defining a disease?

Forgive me for sitting on the sidelines and watching the news from the bleachers. What I'm going to talk about is not the event, but the aftershock.

The American Medical Association [AMA] officially classified obesity as a *"disease state with multiple pathophysiological aspects requiring a range of interventions,"* a hotly debated change that follows in the footsteps of the American Association of Clinical Endocrinologists (2012) and the Obesity Society (2008) and highly supported by the American College of Cardiology and the American Heart Association.

It wasn't a shoo-in: The AMA committee appointed to the task recommended *against* the disease classification, but the AMA House of Delegates—the providers—overruled that recommendation and passed the motion with a large (no pun intended) majority (276–181—60.4% to 39.6%).

The professionals arguing against the classification fell back on the same old sorry party line—there are no specific conditions associated with obesity and that it is a risk factor for other diseases but nothing more.

The AMA made a kind and accurate comparison to other lifestyle-related diseases: *"The suggestion that obesity is not a disease but rather a consequence of a chosen lifestyle exemplified by overeating and/or inactivity is equivalent to suggesting that lung cancer is not a disease because it was brought about by individual choice to smoke cigarettes."* Or diet and hypertension, or alcohol and cirrhosis, or sex and HIV, or drugs and Hepatitis C, or motorcycle accidents and brain injury, among others. We are imperfect beings and we seek physical experience, sometimes to excess and to our detriment.

When they declared obesity a disease, you may have heard me doing my happy dance in my office where I practice functional medicine and integrative psychiatry and treat obesity daily. Finally, I thought, recognition that obesity is *not* simple thermodynamics of calories in = calories burned. If it was that simple, everyone who ever lost weight would still be thin.

Not Everyone Is Happy with the New Classification

I was stunned at the subsequent backlash that occurred, especially since all of the scientific evidence over the last decade points toward obesity as a progressive metabolic, endocrine, toxic, nutritional, psychiatric and inflammatory disease that sabotages weight loss efforts, no matter what the diet. Why would you NOT want obesity classified as a disease?

On Twitter, hashtag "#IAMNOTADISEASE" took over with a vengeance. The fat advocates blogged until they ran out of ink. People worried about the new obesity disease classification as (1) being more stigmatizing than being fat in a supposedly thin society, (2) over-medicalizing obesity because not everyone who is obese is unhealthy, (3) catering to the pharmaceutical and device industry, (4) being inaccurate because there is debate about body mass index as an inaccurate and fallible measure of obesity, and (5) promoting racial discrimination based on the epidemiology of obesity.

Let me try and answer their concerns.

Re: Stigmatization: People were offended and suspicious, especially the community of fat advocates. Apparently the word "disease" is worse than the word "fat." I'm not sure how an already stigmatized condition can be further stigmatized, but I understand how an oppressed group may be overly sensitive to any slight or comment that seems derogatory.

Re: Over-medicalizing: Sigh. I understand that part of fat stigma has been the Health at Every Size (HAES) campaign, which includes healthy eating and movement and a healthy balanced lifestyle, all of which I support and work with my patients daily to achieve. At any size. However, the scientific physiological data just doesn't support long-term "healthy obesity" on a micro or macroscopic level. Fat cells are metabolically active and too many of them are eventually harmful. Years of morbid obesity will eventually erode joints and take a toll on organ systems. Maybe the advocates need to change the term to "healthy obesity at this moment, but maybe not in 20 or 30 or 40 years."

Re: Industry Profit: Yes. Assuming the pharmaceutical and device industries and the supplement industry and the medical and nutritional and even organic food industries will benefit is a given. They all always find a way. But the argument about the pharmaceutical industry making money off fat people is just simply a cost shift from the multibillion-dollar supplement industry that victimizes the gullible and the desperate among us.

Re: Disagreement within the medical and scientific community: There will always be disagreement within the medical community on disease and treatment—that is the definition of evolution. In a brilliant *Aeon* magazine essay, "The Obesity Era," science writer David Berreby said this, "One possible response, of course, is to decide that no obesity policy is possible, because 'science is undecided.' But this is a moron's answer: science is never completely decided. It is *always* in a state of change and self-questioning and it offers no final answers."

Re: Racial Discrimination: Absolutely, I give a nod that poverty is indeed associated with obesity in the United States. . . . In other countries, it is the middle and upper classes that are associated with obesity (such as India). I'm hoping that underserved populations will be able to see professionals about their weight and have it covered, instead of not being able to afford a diet program or a gym. In my real dreams, there are urban community gardens and decent produce and quality protein and fresh fruit in the food deserts and safe areas to exercise or walk. The causal paradox of hunger and cheap food and obesity are not being ignored by classifying obesity as a disease. To the contrary, this reclassification calls attention to *all* causes of obesity—physiological, psychological, social, environmental, genetic, hormonal and economic.

So what is this about?

Maybe, just maybe, calling obesity a disease implies it is hopeless.

So let's look at the actual AMA proclamation and how it is helpful, not hopeless.

Is Obesity Really a Disease?

The AMA says these are the "common criteria in defining a disease: 1) an impairment of the normal functioning of some aspect of the body; 2) characteristic signs or symptoms; and 3) harm or morbidity."

Re: Impaired physiologic functioning: "There is now an overabundance of clinical evidence to identify obesity as a multi-metabolic and hormonal disease state including impaired functioning of appetite dysregulation, abnormal energy balance, endocrine dysfunction including elevated leptin levels and insulin resistance, infertility, dysregulated adipokine signaling, abnormal endothelial function and blood pressure elevation, nonalcoholic fatty liver disease, dyslipidemia and systemic and adipose tissue inflammation."

Re: Characteristic signs and symptoms: "Including the increase in body fat and symptoms pertaining to the accumulation of body fat, such as joint pain, immobility, sleep apnea and low self-esteem."

Re: Associated harm or morbidity: "The physical increase in fat mass associated with obesity is directly related to comorbidities including type 2 diabetes, cardiovascular disease, some cancers, osteoporosis, polycystic ovary syndrome."

In my opinion, the AMA made the case for obesity as a disease. It gets even worse scientifically. In a groundbreaking study published in *PLoS One* 6/26/2013, *overweight* may be a disease also. In a study of 200,000 people affected by a common genetic variant, even a *one unit* increase in BMI [body mass index] is associated with a 20 percent increased risk of developing heart failure. Further, the study also confirms that obesity leads to higher insulin values, higher blood pressure, worse cholesterol values, increased inflammation markers and increased risk of diabetes.

How Does Classifying Obesity as a Disease Help Patients and Providers?

How does a disease classification help providers and patients give and receive treatment and help?

1) *Insurance Coverage.* In my world, a diagnosis of morbid obesity is not yet reimbursable. I find myself having to scratch out an explanation of an eating disorder or anxiety or irritable bowel syndrome to cover the time and appointments that are needed for someone to completely change their lifestyle. In addition, prescription medications that are sometimes helpful will be covered, as will surgeries for people who need drastic measures to prevent end-stage disease *before they develop those diseases.* Patients with obesity will be able to see the dietitian or nutritionist, unlike the present where those appointments are not covered unless you already have diabetes and then, only once a year. Losing weight requires a great deal of support—people should be able to see their professionals as often as needed. And maybe, in an ideal world, physical therapy will be expanded to include physical fitness.

2) *Reducing Weight Bias Among Health Care Providers.* One fact to consider is that currently many, if not most, physicians and medical students and nurses and other health care providers are biased against obese patients. Interestingly, health care professionals also freely admit they have no skill or training or knowledge in how to treat these patients' obesity other than treating the associated late-stage diseases. We providers don't like it when we have no idea what to do for someone. A formal disease classification opens the medical school curriculum floodgates with research, algorithms, evidence and support.

3) *Politics, Policy and Funding.* The AMA decision does not have legal clout, but becomes a central reference point for legislators and policy makers and funders when setting medical policy and health regulations and determining funding priorities. Honestly? I dislike the politicians legislating medical care as much as anyone, but at this point, I dislike lip service for obesity more. Fund us and let us go to work.

How Does Obesity as a Disease Benefit the Holistic Practitioner?

Easy. The more we learn, the more we have to offer. We're currently working off of minimal research and findings, with a great deal of mainstream opposition. Remember the position of acupuncture 25 years ago? Now . . . acupuncture is totally mainstream and covered by many insurers. We are in the early years with alternative obesity treatment. There is a dearth of substantial credible data and we are relying mostly on observational or exploratory data or small studies lacking statistical power. And yet we know from those patients, one at a time, who have responded, that many alternative treatments have potential in the treatment of obesity.

Weight loss coach Steve Nicander, who lost 400 pounds through lifestyle changes and promotes a holistic weight loss program, "Healthful Hope," expresses this beautifully. Says

Steve, "I may have lost a massive amount of weight, but in my mind I will always consider myself to be obese and have that potential to be again. What I think this will do is allow for better treatment methods starting with our chronic childhood obesity problem, allowing them to feel more comfortable discussing it with their health care providers. I hope the best and biggest change coming from this new awareness is improved training in medical schools in dealing with this epidemic, where education is at a bare minimum. Holistic approaches and non-invasive measures, as you know, can still reverse the weight and cure the underlying diseases."

Nothing works for everyone, but most treatments work on someone. Lately, I'm relying on my new pulsed electromagnetic stimulation device and running the obesity program to see if I lose weight with the same lifestyle (which is pretty organic but a little under-exercised and overworked). At the same time, I'm happy to share the latest animal data on green coffee beans which demonstrates absolutely no weight gain prevention. I feel like I'm pitching blindfolded. It's not enough. I need more and just like the commercial with those adorable kids . . . I WANT MORE. The door just creaked open.

| "It would be as false to say that everyone who is obese is sick as to say that every normal-weight person is well."

The AMA's Classification of Obesity as a Disease Is a Mistake

Richard Gunderman

In the following viewpoint, Richard Gunderman argues that it was a mistake for the American Medical Association (AMA) to classify obesity as a disease because there are obese people whose lives are neither negatively affected nor shortened by it—some of whom he names—while many normal-weight people do not stay healthy. He points out that although obesity is a risk factor for some diseases, there are diseases for which overweight people are at low risk. It is impossible, he says, to tell from a person's weight what lies ahead in terms of health for that person. Gunderman is a physician and professor at Indiana University, where he is vice chair of the Radiology Department.

As you read, consider the following questions:

1. What health conditions does Gunderman mention for which normal-weight people are at higher risk than those who are overweight?

2. Why does Gunderman consider body mass index (BMI) a poor method of defining obesity?

3. What was the result of Denmark's short-lived tax on fatty foods?

Last week [in June 2013] at the annual meeting of the American Medical Association [AMA] in Chicago, the organization's delegates voted for the first time to designate obesity a disease. How should the rest of us respond? When we meet obese people, should we cast them a knowing glance of concern and ask how they are doing? Should we send flowers and "get well soon" cards to obese family members and friends?

Should the U.S. declare war on obesity, as we once did on cancer?

If obesity truly is a disease, then over 78 million adults and 12 million children in America just got classified as sick. Their ranks have included a number of prominent people, such as actors John Goodman and Kathy Bates, musicians B.B. King and Aretha Franklin, politicians Al Gore and Newt Gingrich, professional athletes John Kruk and Charles Barkley, media personalities Oprah Winfrey and Michael Moore, and Microsoft CEO [chief executive officer] Steve Ballmer. Everyone has friends and acquaintances who now qualify as diseased.

Yet many sensible people, from physicians to philosophers, know that declaring obesity a disease is a mistake. Simply put, obesity is not a disease. To be sure, it is a risk factor for some diseases. But it would be as false to say that everyone who is obese is sick as to say that every normal-weight person is well. Hence the AMA's vote raises some key questions. Why did it take this action? What is problematic about treating obesity as a disease? And how should sensible people think about obesity?

One reason for naming obesity a disease is the fact that being markedly overweight is positively correlated with a variety of health problems. Some of these problems are risk factors for diseases, such as hypertension, abnormal blood lipid levels, and sleep apnea. Others are diseases in their own right, such as heart attack, stroke, gallbladder disease, and osteoarthritis. Obesity is also a risk factor for some cancers, including those of the endometrium, breast, and colon.

Another reason for declaring obesity a disease is financial. It will nudge health care payers, including private insurers and the federal government, to pay for anti-obesity services, including weight loss counseling and programs. Why, proponents ask, should we pay physicians and hospitals tens of thousands of dollars to open blocked arteries yet refuse to spend a fraction of this amount on diet and fitness programs that might prevent the problem in the first place?

Not All Obese People Get Sick

Yet everyone who is obese does not get sick, and many normal-weight people do not stay healthy. I have known slim and trim people who took scrupulous care of themselves throughout their lives yet fell ill and died young. Others who exhibited no particular interest in their health and did not watch their weight lived to a ripe old age. In most cases, we simply cannot tell from a person's weight what lies ahead for them in life.

Consider Winston Churchill. Though average in height, Churchill weighed upwards of 250 pounds. He smoked cigars. He drank relatively heavily. He did not jog or work out. Yet he became perhaps the most important statesman of the 20th century and one of the greatest political orators in history. He served twice as Britain's prime minister, guiding his nation through a particularly perilous chapter in its history, and won the Nobel Prize for literature. He lived to age 90.

Fat May Be a Symptom of Disease Rather than Its Cause

Despite much speculation, very little evidence has been produced regarding the question of exactly how adiposity is supposed to cause disease. With the exception of osteoarthritis, where increased body mass contributes to wear on joints, and a few cancers where estrogen originating in adipose tissue may contribute, causal links between body fat and disease remain hypothetical. It is quite possible, and even likely, that higher than average body fat is merely an expression of underlying metabolic processes that themselves may be the sources of the pathologies in question. For example, much evidence suggests that insulin resistance is a product of an underlying metabolic syndrome that also predisposes persons to higher adiposity because compensatory insulin secretion promotes fat storage. Modern molecular genetics confirms the thrifty gene hypothesis that mutations favouring fat storage and survival of famine also confer risk of diabetes. Thus, obesity may be an early symptom of diabetes rather than its underlying cause.

Paul Campos, Abigail Saguy, Paul Ernsberger,
J. Eric Oliver, and Glenn Gaesser, "The Epidemiology of
Overweight and Obesity: Public Health Crisis or Moral Panic?,"
International Journal of Epidemiology, *vol. 35, February 2006.*

Thinner isn't always better. A number of epidemiological studies have concluded that normal-weight people are in fact at higher risk of some diseases, including cardiovascular disease, compared to those who are overweight. And there are health conditions for which being overweight is actually protective. For example, heavier women are less likely to develop osteoporosis than thin women. Likewise, among the elderly, being somewhat overweight is often an indicator of good health.

Of even greater concern is the fact that obesity turns out to be very difficult to delineate. It is often defined in terms of body mass index, or BMI. BMI equals body mass divided by the square of height. An adult with a BMI of 18 to 25 is often considered to be normal weight. Between 25 and 30 is overweight. And over 30 is considered obese. Obesity, in turn, can be divided into moderately obese (30 to 35), severely obese (35 to 40), and very severely obese (over 40).

While such numerical standards seem straightforward, they are not. Obesity is probably less a matter of weight than body fat. Some people with a high BMI are in fact extremely fit, while others with a low BMI may be in poor shape. For example, many collegiate and professional football players qualify as obese, though their percentage body fat is low. By BMI, Dwayne "The Rock" Johnson is obese. Conversely, someone with a small frame may have high body fat but a normal BMI.

Attitudes Toward Obesity Vary

Today we have a tendency to stigmatize obesity. The overweight are sometimes pictured in the media with their faces covered. Stereotypes associated with obesity include laziness, lack of will power, and lower prospects for success. Teachers, employers, and health professionals have been shown to harbor biases against the obese. Even very young children tend to look down on the overweight, and teasing about body build has long been a problem in schools.

Negative attitudes toward obesity, grounded in health concerns, have stimulated a number of anti-obesity policies. My own hospital system has banned sugary drinks from its facilities, making it impossible to purchase a non-diet soft drink there. Many employers have instituted weight loss and fitness initiatives. Michelle Obama has launched a high-visibility campaign against childhood obesity, even telling Dr. Oz that it represents our greatest national security threat.

The track record of governmental anti-obesity initiatives is mixed at best. One of the most widely reported was Denmark's so-called "fat tax," which consisted of a surcharge on all foods with a saturated fat content greater than 2.3 percent. The result? Danes switched to lower-cost versions of the same foods and began doing more of their shopping internationally, making their purchases in fat-tax-free countries. The fat tax lasted about a year before it was repealed.

In many cultures throughout history and even today, plump has been preferred to thin. Consider, for example, Shakespeare's Falstaff or the paintings of Peter Paul Rubens. In a community full of people who struggle to get enough to eat, being well fed and having a well-fed family is often a sign of success. A hearty appetite generally indicates health and may even suggest that a person knows how to enjoy life.

This reminds me of a story about Herman Wells, the long-time president and chancellor of Indiana University. Wells was obese from childhood throughout his adult life. In preparation for minor surgery, his physician once advised him to lose 20 pounds. "That's easy," Wells replied. "I have done that dozens of times." Wells accepted his weight. He did not torture himself about it. In fact, he could even laugh about it, and he did so throughout all 97 years of his full life.

Is obesity bad for people? For some, especially patients who are extremely overweight, the answer is almost certainly yes. Would many overweight people benefit from exercising more and eating less? Again, the answer is likely yes. But this does not make obesity a disease. Many people are not harmed by carrying extra pounds, some may actually benefit from it, and we have yet to define it authoritatively. For these reasons, we should think twice before labeling obese people diseased.

> "We should extend to persons with obesity the same respect that we extend to those suffering from other chronic diseases."

Obesity Fits Any Reasonable Definition of Disease

Scott Kahan

In the following viewpoint, Scott Kahan argues that obesity is a chronic medical condition and therefore a disease. In his opinion, few people would disagree, if they were not prejudiced against obese people because of their appearance. He lists the characteristics of a disease according to its dictionary definition and maintains that obesity has all of these characteristics. Obesity is usually dismissed as the result of unhealthy behavior, he says, but people who are not obese also have unhealthy lifestyles, and when they get sick as a result of their behavior, they are not blamed and ridiculed as obese people are. He believes obese persons are entitled to just as much support. Kahan is a public health physician and director of the National Center for Weight and Wellness, as well as a member of the Johns Hopkins Weight Management Center staff.

As you read, consider the following questions:

1. According to Kahan, what are the causes of obesity?

2. What similarities does Kahan see between obesity, high blood pressure, and type 2 diabetes?

3. How, according to Kahan, are people with obesity treated differently from people with other diseases?

By now, virtually everyone reading this is familiar with the alarming stats on obesity rates and the health outcomes associated with excess weight. And by now, we've all had a chance to develop our own opinions about *what obesity is* and why most of us are getting fat. Here's mine:

Obesity is a chronic medical condition—i.e., a *disease*.

And few people would disagree with me . . . if we all weren't so blinded by the sight of heavy people.

Let's assume, for a moment, that obesity was not associated with having excess weight. That is, imagine if eating too much led to all the health consequences of obesity, such as elevated cholesterol, "hardening" of the arteries, enlargement of the heart, growth of cancerous cells—but not an overt and outward gaining of weight. *If we were blind to the aesthetics of obesity, would anyone fail to see it as a disease?*

From a technical perspective, obesity fits any reasonable definition of disease. According to my medical dictionary, a disease is:

An impairment of the body or one of its parts resulting from various causes, such as infection, genetic defect, or environmental stress, and characterized by an identifiable group of signs or symptoms. Let's see . . .

. . . an impairment of the body. *Check.* Obesity goes way beyond its outward appearance. Most affected people develop a cluster of metabolic, hormonal and cellular disruptions—so much so that having obesity increases the risk of dozens of other chronic diseases, and ultimately premature death.

. . . resulting from various causes. *Check.* Obesity doesn't just "happen." It usually results from a constellation of drivers (genetics, environment, medical disorders, stress and many others) that interact with our conscious decision-making processes, leading to the consumption of more calories than are "burned off" by movement and metabolism.

. . . characterized by an identifiable group of signs or symptoms. *Check.* Weight gain, difficulty moving, diminished breathing capacity, skin changes, joint pain, to name a few.

A disease is a *dis-ease* of a part of the body. Clinical depression is a disease. So is a broken bone. So is severe acne. And so is obesity. That most people generally don't define these as diseases is a matter of convention, not fact.

Medically, obesity is no different from other chronic diseases. Consider the similarities between obesity, hypertension ("high blood pressure"), and type 2 diabetes:

- Each involves malfunctions of intricately regulated systems: blood pressure in the case of hypertension, blood sugar in the case of diabetes and energy balance and body weight in the case of obesity.

- Each has significant genetic predispositions and can ultimately result in serious health consequences.

- Each is associated with unhealthy diets and physical inactivity. This is essential to appreciate. The eating and inactivity patterns that lead to excess weight gain in susceptible people are the same ones that lead to chronic diseases in others—even in "skinny" people.

The National Institutes of Health, the World Health Organization and numerous other scientific organizations regard obesity as a disease, yet most people continue to dismiss obesity as a "willful misconduct" and label people who have obesity as lazy and weak.

Not All Obese People Benefit from Weight Loss

An important question that seems to be unresolved is whether MHO [metabolically healthy obese] individuals would gain any metabolic benefit from weight loss. Indeed, several studies have shown that weight loss improves insulin sensitivity and metabolic abnormalities and reduces the risk for type 2 diabetes in obese individuals. However, attempts to achieve weight loss in MHO individuals, by way of diet, may be actually counterproductive and potentially harmful. One may even question the need to aggressively treat MHO individuals given their favourable metabolic profile. . . .

Our results suggest that MHO individuals may respond differently to an energy-restricted diet compared with at-risk individuals who achieve a similar weight loss, in that insulin sensitivity significantly improved in at-risk participants, but significantly deteriorated in MHO individuals in response to the 6 month diet. . . . A better understanding of MHO individuals has important implications for medical education and research. It is important to educate health care professionals and physicians regarding the different needs of subsets of obese individuals. The tendency to treat obese individuals with a 'one size fits all' approach may be counterproductive in the MHO individual.

A.D. Karelis, V. Messier, M. Brochu, and R. Rabasa-Lhoret, "Metabolically Healthy but Obese Women: Effect of an Energy-Restricted Diet," Diabetologia, vol. 51, May 27, 2008.

Sure, there's an element of choice—personal decisions and behaviors are a central piece of most chronic diseases. But poor food and physical activity decisions aren't exclusive to people with obesity. It's just that we plainly see evidence of their unhealthy behaviors—on their bellies and hips and thighs—whereas thin people wear their unhealthy decisions on the inside, hidden from scrutiny.

In fact, the vast majority of Americans, regardless of weight, are eating unhealthily and barely moving. In many cases, people with obesity aren't eating worse or moving less than skinny people. Yet while we instinctively comfort and support normal-weight persons who suffer from hypertension or diabetes or other chronic diseases, even though unhealthy eating and inactivity were likely involved in developing those diseases, we ridicule and punish persons with obesity. Even doctors aren't immune to this stigma.

Such misperceptions and prejudices get in the way of our collective ability to fully understand, prevent and treat this disease.

We should extend to persons with obesity the same respect that we extend to those suffering from other chronic diseases—including access to appropriate and evidence-based treatments. Doing so doesn't negate the importance of taking a central role in managing their health any more than prescribing blood pressure medications to persons with hypertension obviates the need for their healthy eating and physical activity.

Most importantly, our focus needs to shift from blame and ridicule to working together to address the "obesogenic" environment, which shapes our personal decisions and health outcomes. Policies and preventive options that address the physical and social environment (such as the economics of food production, access to healthy foods, junk food marketing and many other factors) to make healthy lifestyle choices the default would benefit everyone, regardless of weight.

> *"People who eat a healthy diet and re-main at a consistent weight are healthy, even if that consistent weight is classi-fied as 'overweight' or even 'obese.'"*

Being Overweight Does Not Always Mean Being Unhealthy

S.E. Smith

In the following viewpoint, S.E. Smith argues that being over-weight is not the same as being unhealthy and that the two are separate issues. She points out that although there are more overweight people in the world than there used to be, this does not mean there is an "epidemic" of unhealthy people. She further maintains that if a person who is overweight can lose weight only by eating a starvation diet, this can cause worse health problems than remaining at that person's natural weight. Smith is a writer and activist who focuses on social justice issues. Her work has appeared in many magazines.

As you read, consider the following questions:

1. What does Smith consider to be a better predictor of health than weight?

2. According to Smith, why are some people who eat a healthy diet still overweight?

3. In Smith's opinion, why do many people maintain that being overweight is always unhealthy?

I was talking to [my friend] Tristan the other day about fat acceptance, and I realized when I was giving him a brief primer on some key points that the fat acceptance movement is still not very good about getting its message out there, and providing information which people can use and think about. It's not just enough to say that people should be accepted, regardless of size: it's necessary to debunk some of the commonly held and erroneous beliefs about size, health, and character.

For starters, straight up, people are getting fatter. I'm not talking about the so-called obesity epidemic, and I'm also ignoring BMI [body mass index]-based statistics, because they are wrong. This is pure numbers, here, people, as in the number of people over 200 pounds, 300 pounds, and so forth. There are more fat people in the world today than there were 10 years ago. That's not something that I am going to try to argue with someone.

That said, though, we need to think about the implications of that fact. A lot of people seem to think that people of weak moral character become fat, and that fat people are automatically unhealthy, and therefore the "epidemic" of fat is an epidemic of unhealthy people. The implication being that we are a drain on the medical system because of our size, and that, furthermore, if we just were *better people*, we wouldn't be so fat. And, of course, if we weren't liars who were in denial about our fat.

Being Fat Is Not Always Unhealthy

So, here's the problem. Fat does not equal unhealthy. In fact, if you want to look at health risks in the respective BMI catego-

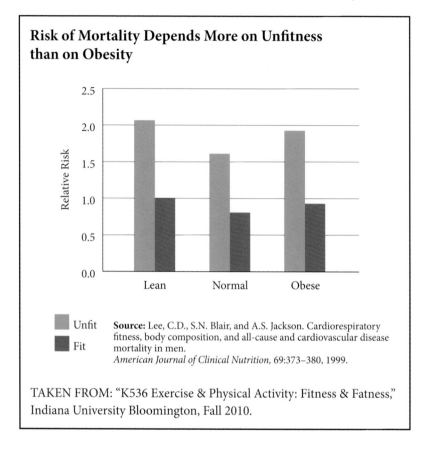

Risk of Mortality Depends More on Unfitness than on Obesity

Relative Risk (y-axis: 0.0, 0.5, 1.0, 1.5, 2.0, 2.5)

Categories: Lean, Normal, Obese

Legend: Unfit, Fit

Source: Lee, C.D., S.N. Blair, and A.S. Jackson. Cardiorespiratory fitness, body composition, and all-cause and cardiovascular disease mortality in men. *American Journal of Clinical Nutrition*, 69:373–380, 1999.

TAKEN FROM: "K536 Exercise & Physical Activity: Fitness & Fatness," Indiana University Bloomington, Fall 2010.

ries, which is the yardstick which most people use when accusing fat people of being disgusting blobs of ill health, I am actually *less* prone to health problems than Tristan is. Numerous studies have shown this, and you can read all about them at places like *Junkfood Science* [a blog].

Being fat is not a disease. Being fat does not necessarily cause disease. And the simplistic assumption that diet and exercise can be used to control weight needs to be thrown out. Yes, diet and exercise *can* play a role in how much someone weighs, as evidenced by the fact that when people like me starve ourselves, we become "normal." (And I mean literally starve, on diets with far fewer calories than those used in starvation studies, and continue to eat at alarmingly low levels once "goal weight" has been achieved.) Being fat has to do with a lot of factors, which can include things like medications, genetics, and stress levels.

You know what's a really good predictor of health? Exercise levels. I don't exercise very much, therefore I am less healthy than I should be. When I do exercise, I am healthier, but not necessarily less heavy. In fact, sometimes I get heavier, because when I exercise, I build muscle. And, guess what, muscle weighs more than fat, including the fat it replaces!

Another good predictor? Diet. You can eat a healthy diet and still be fat, because a healthy diet is not equal to a starvation diet, and every body has a set point. People who fight with their weight repeatedly and yo-yo radically between weights can actually incur serious health problems. People who eat a healthy diet and remain at a consistent weight are healthy, even if that consistent weight is classified as "overweight" or even "obese" under the highly flawed BMI measure.

Cholesterol levels are another pretty darn good measure and a great assessment of the risk of developing cardiovascular disease. So are, according to some studies, the distributions of fat on the body; people with so-called "visceral fat" appear to be more prone to health problems, no matter what their weight may be.

I think that people decide that fat must equal unhealthy because they can hide behind the health argument when they are confronted with the fat acceptance movement. It's easier to say that fat people are unhealthy than it is to openly admit that you think fat people are disgusting. And that's why I make it a point to educate people about the need to decouple fat and health, because they are separate issues.

It's also easier to avoid confronting your own prejudice when you can simply accuse fat people of being lazy and stupid. When you can say that we must be lying when we report how much we eat, and how much we exercise, because *obviously* you would never get *that fat* unless you were chowing down on cheeseburgers constantly. And, of course, when you see actual visual illustrations of what people of different heights and weights look like, you might be surprised about how your perceptions of "fat" change.

*"By acknowledging obesity as a disease,
the AMA is placing obesity on par with
the same diseases that sick fat cells create."*

Calling Obesity a Disease
Will Force Awareness That
Being Obese Impairs Health

Wendy Scinta

*In the following viewpoint, Wendy Scinta expresses surprise that
the American Medical Association's (AMA's) decision to call obesity a disease has aroused criticism. She declares that it was right
because in her opinion there is no such thing as a healthy obese
person. She argues that fat cells are damaging whether or not a
person is ill. She feels that the fact that obesity has been labeled
a disease will force both obese and non-obese individuals, as well
as physicians, to change their attitudes toward it. Scinta, a physician, is the chief medical officer and an advisory board member for 3Pound Health, a commercial enterprise that aims to
help individuals lose weight by changing their behavior.*

As you read, consider the following questions:

1. Why, in Scinta's opinion, are obese people unhealthy
   even if they have not been diagnosed with any illness?

2. What effect does Scinta believe calling obesity a disease will have on national organizations for supporting people with chronic illnesses?

3. Why does Scinta think calling obesity a disease will have an impact on agriculture?

On Tuesday, June 18, 2013, the American Medical Association [AMA] officially recognized obesity as a disease. As an obesity medicine specialist intimately involved in this battle, I never expected this decision to be met with such apathy.

Since the landmark decision, a flurry of accusations have occurred:

- The AMA has been accused of making the decision with the sole purpose of profiting from pharmaceutical companies.

- Obese individuals have been blamed for creating another reason to ignore personal accountability.

- Obesity advocates have been charged by fat activists of increasing stigma for obese individuals (the very people they advocate for) by supporting this decision.

Why so much finger-pointing?

The implications of this ruling are greater than many of us can comprehend. By acknowledging obesity as a disease, the AMA is placing obesity on par with the same diseases that sick fat cells create: diabetes, hypertension, high cholesterol, and heart disease. With obesity legitimized, we are all forced to change the way we think. But is America ready?

For an obese individual, classifying obesity as a disease forces you to view yourself differently. There is no such thing as a healthy obese person. Even if you do not have a formal diagnosis of diabetes, hypertension, or high cholesterol, you are not immune to the mass effects of fat itself: arthritis in the weight-bearing joints, chronic back pain, gastric reflux disease, sleep apnea, vascular compromise, skin problems and right-sided heart failure. Even the strongest frame cannot offset such mechanical stress.

Examining Biases

Declaring obesity a disease causes non-obese Americans to look into their own biases. One blogger wrote, "Does this mean that I can call in 'fat' to work now?" It is easier to ostracize than make the effort to educate oneself about the complexity of obesity. Even a small weight gain can cause dysfunctional or "sick" fat cells. These cells produce more than 100 chemicals, some of which make it extremely difficult for an individual to feel a sense of fullness—which feeds the rolling snowball of weight gain. Are non-obese Americans willing to accept that obesity is more than just a character flaw?

Legitimizing obesity forces the medical community to face our own weight issues and biases. The Physicians' Health Study showed that 44% of male physicians are overweight. Despite this, we are some of the harshest critics of our obese patients. The AMA's ruling should provide an opportunity to teach students, residents, and practicing physicians how to treat obesity effectively and with compassion. We will also need a paradigm shift. Instead of Band-Aiding obesity with medications for the affected illnesses, physicians will need to learn how to treat the core issue, i.e., the dysfunctional fat. Our focus will then shift from disease treatment to reversal and prevention. Are physicians ready for this?

Disease reversal is going to force national organizations that profit from chronic diseases to redefine their roles. Speaking at the American Diabetes Association EXPO in New York City, I was pulled aside by another speaker and reprimanded for discussing how weight loss could reverse type 2 diabetes. "We don't talk about reversing diabetes here," I was told. Are such organizations, and their constituents, ready to put patients ahead of the money and be honest with them about what truly works? Calling obesity a disease will also highlight our completely dysfunctional agriculture system. The obesity epidemic coincides with the loss of diversification of agriculture, and the increase in production of high-fructose corn syrup. It also mirrors the increased production of highly palatable processed foods. The sizable cost disparity between healthy and unhealthy foods continues to grow. Changing this will require a complete overhaul of our agriculture policies. Is the government ready for this?

Obesity costs the U.S. $190 billion per year, 21% of total health care costs, 4–5% of our GDP [gross domestic product]. It affects 33% of adults, and 17% of children in this country with no end in sight. So, does America want to solve the obesity epidemic? It is no longer a question of want, but rather an impending need. We are in a crisis. The economic and human toll from obesity is past its tipping point. There is no longer time for denial, drama, resentment, finger-pointing and Band-Aids to fix this issue. We must make big changes in our communities, our government, and in our individual lives to resolve this epidemic *now*.

| "How is simply declaring me as diseased based on statistics, and despite how I feel or the quality of my life, good for my health?"

Calling Obese Individuals Diseased on the Basis of Statistics Is Wrong

Kath Read

In the following viewpoint, Kath Read, a fat acceptance activist, expresses how angry she is about the American Medical Association's (AMA's) classification of obesity as a disease. She describes how depressed she was to be devalued and called defective, as if she were merely something to be eradicated, on the basis of mere statistics. The decision to call obesity a disease ignores her own feelings about being fat, she declares, and disregards individual quality of life. Read is an Australian activist in the fat acceptance movement, which holds that people are of various sizes and should not be judged on that basis.

As you read, consider the following questions:

1. In Read's opinion, why did the AMA classify obesity as a disease?

2. According to Read, why is the labeling of an obese person as diseased too arbitrary?

3. What makes Read feel defective even though she does not believe it is bad to be overweight?

One of the things about being a highly visible, deeply combative fat activist is that everyone seems to think you're made of steel. That you are so strong and confident, that nothing ever hurts you or makes you feel bad. Nobody believes that you have bad days, that there are times where the fight just goes out of you and you can't face another moment of trying to claw your way out of the hatred and stigma that surrounds fat people.

But that's not true. It's not true in the slightest. Even the most radical fatty, the most sartorially brave, the fiercest fighter, the strongest critic of the dominant paradigm around fatness struggles. Every single one of us have those times where we just run out of oomph.

I am having one of those days today, and have been really struggling all afternoon. You see, the American Medical Association [AMA] today declared obesity as a disease despite a report from their own council on science and public health urging them not to. According to the AMA, we fat people are no longer just people, we are diseased, defective, damaged, broken. We are officially diseases to be cured, prevented, eradicated. And this news has shaken me to the core. I simply feel so defeated right now, like all the work that I and many other fat activists have done, and are doing, to claw back our rights and improve our quality of life has just been taken away from us.

The Ruling Was Made for Financial Profit

Rationally, I know why the AMA has made this ruling. They've done so because big pharmaceutical companies, the weight loss industry and big health insurance companies, have lobbied, threatened, bullied and bribed them to do so. Rationally

The Last Acceptable Prejudice

People who look different, by choice or not, are often the subject of preconceived negative attitudes—they are defined as "Other," as somehow not human. . . .

The reason fat is called the last acceptable prejudice is that even many social justice advocates believe that fat individuals deserve the stigma they face. Where a joke about a little person or a racial slur will get you chastised by a social justice advocate, fat prejudice and oppression are seldom questioned. . . . Far too many people who put themselves in the social justice category believe that fat individuals deserve the treatment they receive. . . .

One day as a society we will understand that fat prejudice, along with all other stigmas, is not acceptable. It is time for Western society to understand that no prejudice is *ever* acceptable. It is time for us to see all people as individuals and none as inhuman "Other." It is time for us to grow up and become a mature, accepting society. . . .

Prejudice, stigma and oppression are not acceptable in enlightened societies, as the United States claims to be. It is time for us to recognize all oppression, even well-hidden oppression, and put a stop to it.

Lonie McMichael, Acceptable Prejudice?: Fat, Rhetoric and Social Justice. *Nashville, TN: Pearlsong Press, 2013.*

I know that the reason these big corporations have done this is because it's in their best interest financially to do so. After all, they're raking in *huge* amounts of money by convincing society in general that appearance = health, and that if you don't meet the arbitrary levels of appearance that you must be sick, and surprise surprise, they have a drug, or a surgery, or a device, or a diet plan or an extra expensive health insurance plan to sell you to fix it. The weight loss industry alone was worth almost $800 million just here in Australia. Can you imagine what could be done for $800 million per year in this country? We could all have completely free health care for every Australian, more than we would ever need. People with disabilities could have all of the equipment that they would ever need, and any support and care they would ever need. No human being in Australia would go without food, water or housing. Education would be free for our whole lives, from kindergarten through any university studies that we would care to take on. Medical research into every known actual disease, from the common cold to cancer could be funded fully.

All this just from the money that the diet and weight loss industry is worth in a single year, and there would be change. In fact, if we only took their profit margin for *one* year, approximately $63 million, and applied that to public funding annually—we could fund a lot of the things I've listed above. And that's just here in Australia, a country of only about 22 million people. In the US, the weight loss industry is worth *66 billion dollars*. Let alone the cumulative value of the rest of the world's weight loss industries.

There is *no way on earth* that the weight loss industry is not behind this ruling from the AMA. They have $66 billion worth of power per annum in the US alone. $66 billion they can spend on lobbying, propaganda, graft, legal threats to anyone who opposes them, you name it to make sure the ruling falls the way they want it to.

Rationally I know this. I know the facts. I've done years of my own research into this because what I was being told about my fat body wasn't matching up to reality.

The Ruling Labels Fat People as Inferior

But despite that knowledge . . . I feel so defeated today. I feel so disheartened. I feel so cheated. I feel like I'm being marked as inferior, defective, broken. Simply because my body happens to fall on the far end of a bell curve of diverse human bodies. Simply because my body doesn't fall in the small peak of the bell curve, the median of human bodies, a tiny arbitrary band of people who are granted the "normal" status just because they're in the middle statistically.

But being at one end of the statistics doesn't reflect who I am. It doesn't reflect how I feel. It doesn't reflect what my body can do. It doesn't reflect my value as a human being. The AMA doesn't know what it feels like to exist in my fat body. They don't know what it's like in my body to wake up after a deep sleep, stretch and feel that stretch go down to my toes and up to my outstretched fingertips. They don't know what it feels like in my body to go swimming, feeling the cool water soft and cocooning around my body, and the wonderful sleepy feeling I get afterwards. They don't know what it feels like in my body to walk along the waterfront near my house on a windy but crystal clear winter day, with the sun warming my back as the wind nips my nose and fingertips. They don't know what it feels like in my body to laugh with my friends, my belly rocking, tears rolling down my face and my ribs hurting from giggling so hard. They don't know anything about what it feels like in my body. All they know is that I am at the far end of a bell curve, and that someone out there can make money from making me hate myself and by encouraging society to hate me, and to repeatedly attempt to move myself to another point on the statistical bell curve, something we scientifically know fails for 95% of all attempts. And with that they have marked me, and people like me, as diseased, defective, broken.

The only time I feel diseased, defective, broken is when society repeatedly pushes me down because of how I look and what numbers show up on a scale when I step on it. I don't feel those things unless I am taught to feel them. Not even when I *actually* suffer illness or injury.

How is simply declaring me as diseased based on statistics, and despite how I feel or the quality of my life, good for my health?

How is that good for anyone's health?

Periodical and Internet Sources Bibliography

The following articles have been selected to supplement the diverse views presented in this chapter.

Christopher Bergland	"Should Obesity Be Classified as a Disease?," *The Athlete's Way—Psychology Today* (blog), June 19, 2013.
Chris Conover	"Declaring Obesity a Disease: The Good, the Bad, the Ugly," *Forbes*, June 28, 2013.
Virginia Hughes	"The Big Fat Truth," *Nature*, May 22, 2013.
Marni Jameson	"'I'm Not a Disease!': In Reclassifying Obesity, AMA Creates Uproar," *Jewish World Review*, June 2013.
Geoffrey Kabat	"Why Labeling Obesity as a Disease Is a Big Mistake," *Forbes*, July 9, 2013.
Christine S. Moyer	"What's Next Now That the AMA Has Declared Obesity a Disease?," *American Medical News*, July 1, 2013.
Anahad O'Connor	"The 'Healthy Obese' and Their Healthy Fat Cells," *Well—New York Times* (blog), October 9, 2013.
Mitchell Roslin	"Yes, Obesity Is a Disease," Live Science, June 19, 2013.
Abigail C. Saguy	"If Obesity Is a Disease, Why Are So Many Obese People Healthy?," *Time*, June 24, 2013.
Marilyn Wann	"The War on Fat People: Doctors Enlist," *Daily Kos*, June 19, 2013.

CHAPTER 3

Should Society Actively Combat Obesity?

Chapter Preface

A common argument for government action to combat obesity is that obesity is widely believed to be extremely costly to society. According to some estimates, obesity-related health care costs up to $190 billion per year. Even allowing for media exaggeration, on the basis of projected health care expenses, it appears that obesity is a drain on the nation's economy.

However, there is another way to look at these figures. Any estimate of the overall cost of treating a specific disease assumes that the people who do not get that disease will never get sick at all. Generally everybody, other than the few who die suddenly, becomes seriously ill sooner or later. Thus the significant factor is not how much expense is incurred by a person's illness, but how much that expense exceeds the average. Journalist Christopher Snowdon in an article titled "The Wages of Sin Taxes" writes, "Cost-of-vice studies only show us costs. They do not show savings. We do not see, for example, the Social Security or Medicare payments and nursing home costs saved by premature mortality. Cost-of-vice studies evaluate health care costs of the average sinner, but these costs are meaningless unless we know the health care costs of the average saint."

A 2009 study reported that in 2006 obese Americans averaged about $1400 more per year in medical costs than non-obese Americans, mostly because a larger percentage of obese individuals had chronic diseases such as diabetes and heart disease. However, this estimate concerned the immediate cost of health care, one year at a time. Studies have shown that when *lifetime* medical and Social Security costs are counted, the rise in obesity costs the public nothing. "Successful prevention of obesity . . . increases life expectancy," writes researcher Pieter van Baal, reporting on a study conducted in the Netherlands. "Unfortunately, these life-years gained are not lived in full health and come at a price: people suffer from other diseases, which increases health-care costs."

Public health issues are often dealt with separately, without any attention given to how expenses balance out. While obesity is one disease about which economists are worried, another disease causing even more worry is the increasing number of people with Alzheimer's disease, a form of dementia that strikes in old age. It has been estimated that nearly half the population over eighty-five will get Alzheimer's disease, which cannot be prevented nor cured and requires long-term nursing care. Although some patients have relatives who can provide this care, many do not, and as of 2012 nursing home care for a person with dementia cost $80,000 to $90,000 per year not covered by health insurance—even more in some localities. The total cost, including medical treatment, is expected to rise from $200 billion in 2012 to over $1 trillion in 2050. Because life expectancy is increasing, the number of dementia patients will grow; however, obesity-related diseases may shorten lives. Therefore, the lifetime cost of care for obese patients may be less than average rather than more. As van Baal wrote, "Obesity prevention may be an important and cost-effective way of improving public health, but it is not a cure for increasing health expenditures."

There are many reasons to aim toward preventing premature illness and death. It is unlikely, however, whether doing so could result in any overall health care cost savings. For this reason, some experts believe that cost-based arguments for government efforts to reduce obesity apply only with respect to short-term costs. The viewpoints in this chapter explore the debate surrounding fighting obesity on a societal level.

> "The so-called 'war on sugar' is not a culture war; it is a public health imperative backed by science."

Public Health Authorities Should Regulate the Sale of Sugary Drinks

Lawrence O. Gostin

In the following viewpoint, Lawrence O. Gostin argues that a ban on the sale of large-size sugary drinks is a necessary public health measure, expressing dismay that a state court blocked such a ban from taking effect in New York City. He disagrees with the objections to it and points out why he considers them invalid. In his opinion, the ban was defeated only because of propaganda from the food and restaurant industries that caused the public and the court to oppose it. Gostin is the director of the World Health Organization's Collaborating Centre on Public Health Law and Human Rights.

As you read, consider the following questions:

1. Why does Gostin believe limiting the size of sugary drinks would reduce obesity?

2. Why, according to Gostin, did the mayor of New York not make the proposed ban on large-size soda apply consistently to all stores and all sugary drinks?

3. What, in Gostin's opinion, gives the New York Board of Health the authority to impose a ban on large-size drinks without the approval of the elected city council?

A state trial judge on Monday [March 11, 2013] blocked New York City's plan for a maximum 16-ounce size for a high-sugar beverage. The ban would have included sodas, energy drinks, fruit drinks and sweetened teas. But it would have excluded alcoholic beverages and drinks that are more than 50% milk, such as lattes. The ban would have applied to restaurants, movie theaters, stadiums and mobile food carts. But it would not have applied to supermarkets and convenience stores, such as 7-Eleven.

Mayor Michael Bloomberg's proposal was met with fierce opposition by the industry and public outrage at the loss of "liberty," the so-called "nanny state" run amok. Beyond all the hype, the industry's vociferous arguments, now adopted by a trial court, are badly flawed.

In fact, the Board of Health has the power, indeed the responsibility, to regulate sugary drinks for the sake of city residents, particularly the poor.

Would the Ban Work?

Nearly six out of 10 New York City residents are overweight or obese, as are nearly four out of 10 schoolchildren. This cannot be acceptable to our society, knowing that obesity is such a powerful risk factor for diabetes, cancer and heart disease. No one would disagree that government should act, but how? There is no single solution, but many ideas that would work in combination. One of those solutions is to control portion size and sugar consumption. Why?

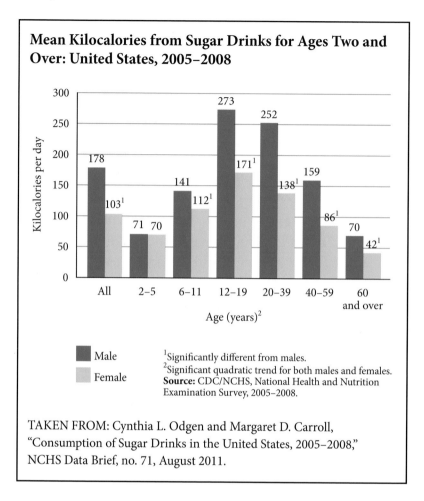

Mean Kilocalories from Sugar Drinks for Ages Two and Over: United States, 2005–2008

Kilocalories per day

- All: Male 178, Female 103[1]
- 2–5: Male 71, Female 70
- 6–11: Male 141, Female 112[1]
- 12–19: Male 273, Female 171[1]
- 20–39: Male 252, Female 138[1]
- 40–59: Male 159, Female 86[1]
- 60 and over: Male 70, Female 42[1]

Age (years)[2]

■ Male
■ Female

[1]Significantly different from males.
[2]Significant quadratic trend for both males and females.
Source: CDC/NCHS, National Health and Nutrition Examination Survey, 2005–2008.

TAKEN FROM: Cynthia L. Odgen and Margaret D. Carroll, "Consumption of Sugar Drinks in the United States, 2005–2008," NCHS Data Brief, no. 71, August 2011.

First, the ever-expanding portions (think "supersized") are one of the major causes of obesity. When portion sizes are smaller, individuals eat less but feel full. This works, even if a person can take an additional portion. (Most won't because they are satiated, and it at least makes them think about what they are consuming.) Second, sugar is high in calories, promotes fat storage in the body and is addictive, so people want more. The so-called "war on sugar" is not a culture war; it is a public health imperative backed by science.

So, there is good reason to believe New York's portion control would work. But why does the city have to prove that it works beyond any doubt? Those who cry "nanny state" in response to almost any modern public health measure (think food, alcohol, firearms, distracted driving) demand a standard of proof that lawmakers don't have to meet in any other field.

When a law is passed to increase jobs, spur the economy or subsidize a corporate sector (oil, for example), we don't insist that lawmakers prove it works. At least public health officials rely on science and try to craft rules that have a chance of working—if not in isolation, then in combination with other obesity control measures such as food labeling, calorie disclosures, trans fat restrictions and access to affordable fruits and vegetables in schools and poor neighborhoods.

Is the Ban Consistent?

The industry stoked the fires of public discontent with its campaign against the "inconsistencies" in the soda ban. Why doesn't the ban apply to milky drinks, why can 7-Eleven sell large sugary drinks, and why not ban refills? Justice Milton Tingling Jr. bought both industry arguments: It won't work and it is inconsistent. He went so far as to call the ban "fraught with arbitrary and capricious consequences" and filled with loopholes. Again, we find a double standard.

Bloomberg did what every other politician does: balance public health and safety with realpolitik. Consider one of the judge's major arguments: balancing public health and economic considerations is "impermissible." This judicial reasoning makes no sense. If policy makers could not balance economic consequences, virtually every law in America would be flawed. There is another huge problem with this argument. It assumes that unless public health does everything, it can do nothing. The whole art of politics is compromise. The mayor gets a lot of what he seeks to fight obesity, but not everything.

Does the Board of Health Have the Power?

Admittedly, the soda ban would have been better coming from the city's elected legislature, the City Council. But the Board of Health has authority to act in cases where there is an imminent threat to health. Doesn't the epidemic of obesity count as an imminent threat, with its devastating impact on health, quality of life and mortality? In any event, the Board of Health has authority over the food supply and chronic disease, which is exactly what it has used in this case.

Members of the Board of Health, moreover, are experts in public health, entitled to a degree of deference. The fact that the proposal originated in the mayor's office does not diminish the board's authority and duty to protect the public's health. Many health proposals arise from the executive branch, notably the [Patient Protection and] Affordable Care Act.

Should Industry Have an Outsized Influence on Public Health Policy?

The fingerprints of the food and restaurant industries, with their clear economic conflicts of interest, are all over the public and judicial campaign to block the soda ban. Industry undertook a multimillion-dollar campaign, flying banners over the city and plastering ads over the subways. They immediately filed suit and hired the most elite law firms.

Rather than recognize the public health effects of large sugary drinks, they chose to fight, reminiscent of Big Tobacco. What is worse, the public (and now a judge) fell for the industry's manipulations. Most New Yorkers oppose the portion ban, while politicians in other states are scrambling to show their disapproval. Mississippi is about to pass a law forbidding portion control. Imagine that in a state with the highest obesity rate in America!

We are used to fierce lobbying for personal gain in America, but that doesn't mean we should be duped by industry propaganda. Is a portion limit really such an assault on freedom? It doesn't stop anyone from buying soda. If consumers really want, they can buy several smaller drinks. It doesn't stop companies from giving refills.

There is really no great burden posed on individuals, only a little nudge in the right direction. At the same time, it could make meaningful changes in the drinking habits of New Yorkers. Why is the industry fighting this so fiercely? Because when it is shown to be successful in New York, it will be emulated in major cities in America and worldwide. Isn't that exactly what we need to stem the tide of obesity?

VIEWPOINT

*"The purpose of government is to pro-
tect freedom, not to heedlessly infringe
upon it merely for the sake of what
some people may believe is doing good."*

Regulating Diet and Health Choices Violates Individual Rights

Jonathan S. Tobin

*In the following viewpoint, Jonathan S. Tobin argues that the
New York City mayor's action in banning the sale of large-size
sodas is a serious violation of individual rights. The purpose of
government, he says, is to protect freedom, not to infringe on it
for the sake of what some people believe will do good. In Tobin's
opinion, whether drinking less soda would be beneficial to health
is not the point, since the right to free choice is more important
than protection from the results of unhealthy choices. Tobin is
the senior online editor of* Commentary *magazine.*

As you read, consider the following questions:

1. What similarity does Tobin see between a ban on large-
   size soda and fascism?

Jonathan S. Tobin, "The Issue Is Freedom, Not Soft Drinks." Reprinted from *Commentary*, May 31, 2013, by permission; copyright © 2013 by Commentary Inc.

2. What danger is there in regulating the sale of soda, in Tobin's opinion?

3. According to Tobin, what would be the result of allowing the mayor to ban private diet choices?

New York City mayor [Michael] Bloomberg struck what he claims is another blow for the cause of public health yesterday [in May 2012] by announcing a ban on the sale of all sugared drinks in containers that measure larger than 16-ounce servings. Because soft drinks are widely believed to be part of the obesity epidemic, he believes it is his duty to try and stop the citizens of Gotham from harming themselves. As the *New York Times* reports:

> "Obesity is a nationwide problem, and all over the United States, public health officials are wringing their hands saying, 'Oh, this is terrible,'" Mr. Bloomberg said in an interview on Wednesday in the Governor's Room at City Hall.
>
> "New York City is not about wringing your hands; it's about doing something," he said. "I think that's what the public wants the mayor to do."

But even if we concede that drinking too much soda is an unhealthy practice, what the mayor again fails to understand is that the purpose of government is to protect freedom, not to heedlessly infringe upon it merely for the sake of what some people may believe is doing good. Like the city's ban on the use of trans fats and draconian restrictions on smoking, the new soda regulations are an intolerable intrusion into the private sphere. Though the mayor seems to relish his reputation as the embodiment of the concept of the so-called nanny state, what is going on here is something far more sinister than a billionaire version of [fictional nanny] Mary Poppins presiding at Gracie Mansion [the official residence of the mayor of New York City]. Rather, it is yet another installment of what [columnist and author] Jonah Goldberg rightly termed "liberal fascism."

© Nate Beeler, "Bloomberg Soda Ban," PoliticalCartoons.com, May 31, 2012.

Though the term "fascist" has become merely a left-wing epithet aimed at non-liberals, its historic roots are in a movement that above all saw the ends as justifying the means. The Italian fascist state of [dictator] Benito Mussolini earned a brief popularity around the world for "making the trains run on time" because his regime appeared to make a chaotic political culture more efficient. But the price paid in terms of freedom for the train timetable was very high. Though Bloomberg is no Mussolini, the underlying principle here is the same. He believes it is his duty to solve any problem even if it means expanding the scope of government to govern personal diet.

Government Has No Right to Regulate Private Choices

The point here is not to defend drinking excessive amounts of soda, consuming trans fats or smoking. It is to point out that these are personal choices that cannot reasonably be interpreted to fall under the purview of municipal government. The danger is that the end of personal liberty is not usually accomplished in one broad stroke but is lost by a process of erosion whereby seemingly sensible measures gradually accumulate to create a new reality wherein the once broad protection of the law for private behavior is destroyed piecemeal.

Those who defend the mayor's actions claim the medical costs of the illnesses caused by drinking, eating and smoking are affected in one way or another by the public and that gives government the right to regulate and/or ban such items. But there is a difference between personal behavior that poses a direct threat to public safety—such as driving while under the influence of alcohol—and those that constitute minute and indirect contributions to serious problems. If the mayor is allowed to ban private diet or health choices under the principle that he has the right to "do something" about anything that is a public concern, then there is literally no limit to his power to infringe on personal liberty or to intrude on commerce.

It may well be that Americans ought not to drink 20-ounce soda bottles any more than they should smoke. But if we are to live in a free country, they must have the right to do so. Those choices have consequences, but so does giving government the power to take those choices away from us. As grievous as our nation's health problems may be, the damage from the latter may far outweigh it.

> "Do people who abuse their bodies through bad eating habits and lack of exercise have the same rights to health services as healthy, fit people who fall ill by chance or accident?"

The Government Should Take Action Against Obesity

Michael Smith

In the following viewpoint, Michael Smith argues that although the idea of government action against obesity conflicts with the principle of free choice, reducing obesity is more important than freedom. He considers the consequences of obesity such a serious threat to the public that it is up to the government to protect people from it, as it would against threats that are not the result of personal behavior. Furthermore, in his opinion, the projected cost of obesity-related disease is so great that action is necessary. Although Smith is writing about Australia, his arguments are equally applicable to America. Smith is the former editor of Australian newspaper the Age.

As you read, consider the following questions:

1. What, in Smith's opinion, are the two most important functions of government?

2. According to Smith, how does mortality from obesity compare with that from historical events that are generally known to have caused many deaths?

3. What actions does Smith believe the government should take to reduce childhood obesity?

The obesity epidemic provides one of the greatest challenges of political philosophy for governments since the birth of democracy. The economic, health and mortality consequences of obesity and its partner diseases are as grave as any crisis faced by any government in history. But most governments are paralysed by the clash of fundamental democratic principles involved.

Since the beginning of civilisation, the two most important functions of government have been to allocate resources and to provide security for the population. On these criteria, obesity demands swift and strong government action. Huge amounts of health dollars are being consumed by the consequences of obesity and the death toll is enormous. The cost is depriving the health system and other services of precious dollars.

Security vs. Freedom

But tough government action runs headlong into another principle of democratic governments—freedom of choice, including the freedom to make unhealthy decisions.

Government security for the people has taken many forms. Initially it was protection from invasion. Later, it included protection from disease through sanitation and a hospital system; protection from criminals through a law enforcement system; and protection from poverty through an income protection system. New priorities can emerge as the threats to a population's security change. For instance, Western governments have put a priority on protection from terrorism following 9/11 [referring to the September 11, 2001, terrorist attacks on the United States].

In the 21st century, the obesity epidemic—together with its downstream manifestations of cardiovascular disease, diabetes and some cancers—is killing more people per year than the annual toll of any war in human history, more people per year than the bubonic plague and the Spanish flu, more people per year than have died in 20 years of AIDS. There are now more overweight and obese people in the world than there are malnourished people.

The cost of obesity in Australia is estimated at $8.3 billion a year and will be a major cause of rising health expenditure in the next 20 years. This means less for schools, education, transport and welfare.

Look to the United States for a window on our [Australia's] future. An American study showed that one-fifth of US health care expenditure would be needed to treat the consequences of obesity by 2020. And there has been a threefold increase in high blood pressure among children in the past 10 years. Ten per cent of American children have high cholesterol.

A major slice of the current generation may not live as long as their parents. And while they survive, they will create a heavier cost burden on society through medications, surgery, consultations and lost productivity.

What is the role of government in stopping this epidemic? Do people who abuse their bodies through bad eating habits and lack of exercise have the same rights to health services as healthy, fit people who fall ill by chance or accident? Should our hospitals be performing obesity quick fixes like gastric-band surgery while there are not enough beds for infant cancer patients? Should unhealthy foods be banned, strictly controlled, taxed more heavily or have their advertising and promotion restricted?

In the context of the two main functions of government (allocation of resources and protecting people from harm), the obesity epidemic should be regarded as a national emergency and should be met with the kind of urgency applied to other emergencies.

Why is this not happening? Obesity is different because it is largely self-inflicted. We know how to fix obesity—eat less and move more. This simple solution relies on personal action. The traditional libertarian argument has been that governments don't belong in people's pantries. And there should be no exercise police.

Government Action Would Be Justified

However, the imperative to tackle obesity is becoming more critical and has been brought into focus by the recent Preventative Health Taskforce report, which recommended measures to force people to make healthier decisions through the tax system and prohibitions on promotion and advertising of unhealthy foods.

[Australian] Health Minister Nicola Roxon seemed to embrace the philosophy of the report when she argued that "we are killing people by not acting". She will now be tested with a palate-cleansing dose of realpolitik.

The public debate has already degenerated into the simplistic and polarising "nanny state" argument. If only it were that simple.

Obesity is overtaking smoking as the leading cause of preventable death. It took almost 50 years from the time that smoking was definitively linked to lung cancer for the full suite of today's wide range of smoking restrictions and taxes to be applied. They worked.

The Australian government, when considering taxes or advertising bans on junk food or meaningful food labelling laws or limits on the amount of fat, salt and sugar in our food, is up against a $100 billion industry concentrated in a few big corporate hands.

Compared to a number of European countries and even the libertarian US, the Australian government has leant much more heavily towards industry self-regulation on big food issues such as trans fats and labelling.

Not All Anti-Obesity Legislation Is Paternalistic

While a desire to improve the health of Americans certainly provides much of the impetus behind anti-obesity legislation, not all such policies can be supported only by an appeal to benevolence. On the contrary, some anti-obesity legislation can be justified by the uncontroversial Millian [referring to John Stuart Mill] harm principle, which contends that government action is justified to prevent and/or redress harm to others.

For example, consider a proposal to institute a "fat tax" on unhealthy fast food, snacks, and soda. While a proponent might justify such a proposal based upon a desire to improve the health of Americans, it could also be supported by a desire to recoup the staggering health care costs currently associated with obesity.... A "fat tax" could therefore be justified without reference to any kind of paternalistic argument....

In addition, relying on Mill's harm principle, one could put forth an argument to end the current subsidies of unhealthy food products, such as the billions of dollars in annual subsidies to grain farmers whose crops ... become cheap ingredients in processed food. The idea would be that such subsidies artificially distort food preferences in an unhealthy direction, leading individuals to consume greater quantities of unhealthy food than they otherwise would....

In sum, several anti-obesity policies that are often characterized as paternalistic are, in fact, nothing of the sort.

Stephen A. McGuinness, "Time to Cut the Fat: The Case for Government Anti-Obesity Legislation," Journal of Law and Health, *vol. 1, no. 1, 2012.*

Effective action will mean balancing competing principles and being decisive about which ones matter most. The government might find this all too hard and the taskforce report will gather dust like so many before it.

The hardheads in the ALP [Australian Labor Party] might see an opportunity created by blatant self-interest. Obesity, smoking and cardiovascular disease rates are significantly higher in lower socioeconomic areas, the Labor heartland. Obesity and related diseases are costing the ALP millions of votes because of premature deaths. And the people likely to be most offended by "nanny state" actions are likely to be those in the blue [conservative] seats anyway.

The obesity epidemic is a failure of family and a failure of government. The point where families and government meet to serve children is in the school system. An enlightened government might decide that the single most important principle is to prevent our children being socialised into bad habits that will diminish and shorten their lives.

An action plan flowing from that principle might include an extended school day to include compulsory physical exercise and nutritional education along with school-supplied breakfast and lunch, thereby providing an economic boost to the healthy food industry and an incentive for our food conglomerates to focus more on big contracts for real food. The children will be fitter and have less time in front of the television, where they are bombarded with dubious nutritional choices. Unless, of course, the government has the courage to act on food advertising.

"Some people who are overweight (and even mildly obese) show no signs of illness. Conversely, lots of thin people out there have heart disease and diabetes."

The War on Obesity Is Unjustified and a Waste of Money

Virginia Hughes

In the following viewpoint, Virginia Hughes explains that obese individuals have been advised to eat less and exercise more for centuries with little effect, and while being obese increases the risk for some diseases, there are many other factors affecting whether or not a person gets sick. Politicians, she says, are not concerned about these other factors; they simply continue to focus on weight, although no weight loss method has been proven to work longer than a year or two. Pointing out that science has shown that weight is largely determined by genetic factors, Hughes questions the wisdom of government action to reduce obesity. Hughes is a science journalist who writes for national magazines.

As you read, consider the following questions:

1. What evidence does Hughes mention for a genetic influence on weight?

2. According to Hughes, is fat tissue in itself known to be harmful?

3. Why does Hughes find the subject of obesity difficult to write about?

Doctors have been telling fat people to eat less and exercise more for at least 2,500 years.

Here's [ancient Greek physician] Hippocrates, father of Western medicine: "It is very injurious to health to take in more food than the constitution will bear, when, at the same time one uses no exercise to carry off this excess."

And here's the blunt advice of Polybus, student (and son-in-law) of Hippocrates: "Persons of a gross relaxed habit or body, the flabby, and red-haired, ought always to use a drying diet. . . . Such as are fat, and desire to be lean, should use exercise fasting; should drink small liquors a little warm; should eat only once a day, and no more than will just satisfy their hunger."

Public health experts no longer disparage red-haired folks, and as far as I know, they don't recommend drinking warmed-up liquors. But they're still spreading the message of the harms of obesity, via television, magazines, school curricula, and even First Lady policy agendas. These efforts have some merit. People who are obese (defined as having a BMI [body mass index] of 30 or higher) have an increased risk of developing heart disease, diabetes and some cancers compared with people who are not obese. And people who are severely obese have a higher death rate than thin people.

The message that thinner = better just seems intuitive, doesn't it? I've certainly heard it all my life (or at least since 3rd grade, when I was mortified to be one of the chubby kids in gym class to *not* get the President's Physical Fitness Award badge) and have never questioned it. But over the past few months, while researching a story published in today's *Nature*, I've started to wonder whether we've gone too far in our cultural war against fat.

Health Risks of Obesity Are Not Clear

Weight is just one factor of many—sleep, diet, fitness, psychological health, socioeconomic status—that influences whether we are healthy or sick. But politicians don't talk about a sleep deprivation epidemic; there is no *Biggest Loser of Poverty* reality TV show.

What's more, the health risks of being "overweight" (defined as a BMI between 25 and 30) are not at all clear. As I describe in depth in the new story, mortality rates of people in the overweight category are actually 6 percent lower than those in the "normal" category, and some people who are overweight (and even mildly obese) show no signs of illness. Conversely, lots of thin people out there have heart disease and diabetes.

Yes, being obese usually takes a toll on health, no question. But guess how many obesity drugs or diet-and-exercise regimes have been proven to last more than a year or two?

Oh, right, zero.

And yet, the battle cry remains: if you're obese, just crank up that willpower! Eat less, move more!

"I would like to believe that modern medicine and modern science can be better than just repeating a 2,000-year-old recommendation," says Jeffrey Friedman, a molecular biologist and trained medical doctor at the Rockefeller University in New York. Friedman has many strong opinions about the so-called obesity "epidemic," which we talked about at length over coffee recently.

Obesity Has Genetic Roots

Friedman has been studying the genetic roots of obesity for more than 30 years. In 1994 he made headlines for the discovery of leptin, a hormone that circulates in blood and turns off hunger signals in the brain. Subsequent studies have found genetic mutations in the leptin gene that cause rare cases of obesity. Twin studies have also shown that obesity has strong genetic roots (it's about as heritable as height, in fact, and yet we don't think of being too short or too tall as some kind of moral failing).

Despite these unquestionable genetic contributions, most of us think of weight as environmentally driven: a direct consequence of a person's personal eating habits. It's this emphasis on behavior that "gives the public a license to stigmatize the obese," Friedman says.

"A lot of people try to couch it in ways that don't as directly lead to stigmatization, but they end up always getting there," Friedman says. "Because you end up saying, at some level, that the obese have made a series of poor choices that have led them to this."

Friedman sees things quite differently, as he eloquently explained in a 2003 commentary in *Science*. Each of us, he argues, has a different genetic predisposition to obesity, shaped over thousands of years of evolution by a changing and unpredictable food supply. In modern times, most people don't have to deal with that nutritional uncertainty; we have access to as much food as we want and we take advantage of it. In this context, some individuals' genetic makeup causes them to put on weight—perhaps because of a leptin insensitivity, say, or some other biological mechanism.

In other words, morbidly obese people lost the genetic lottery. "The irony is, it's the people who are the most obese who are stigmatized the most, and in fact, they're the people who can do the least about it," Friedman says.

The Cost of Obesity

A common argument for treating obesity as a public health problem appeals to the social costs that obese people are said to impose on others. The two most relevant costs are the financial burden obese people may impose on other taxpayers or members of an insurance pool, and decreased average productivity among obese workers.

The issue of external costs is a little more complicated, however, than some have suggested. For one thing, it is important to distinguish the annual costs of obesity from lifetime costs. Although obese people generally impose a higher burden on shared medical resources in any given year, it is conceivable that because obese people live shorter lives, they contribute more than they take away from common medical resources over a lifetime. There is now fairly good evidence that this is true for smokers, and at least one study in Holland suggests the same is true for obesity. If it turns out to be true that obese people provide a net social benefit for shared medical resources, the argument from social cost fails. In fact, it may be used to justify government subsidies rather than taxes for cigarettes and junk food.

Jonny Anomaly, *"Is Obesity a Public Health Problem?,"*
Public Health Ethics, *vol. 5, no. 3, 2012.*

Science Does Not Know Why Obesity Varies

Environment is important, of course: No one, no matter what their genome looks like, can become obese without food. But scientists don't know most of the details of how the environment interacts with genes to control our eating habits. They don't know why this system has such extreme variability in the human population. They don't know why a (very select) few obese people can lose 50 percent of their weight and maintain that loss for decades. And, as I found in my story, researchers definitely don't know why extra weight leads to sickness in some people but not in others. (It's not even clear that fat tissue itself is harmful; it could just be an innocuous by-product of a harmful diet, say, or of not exercising enough.)

This whole subject is steeped in political controversy and a wide array of financial interests, which has made it difficult for me to write about and to think about. But I've tried to be provocative in this post. Considering the economic and cultural investment we've put into the war on obesity, doesn't the public deserve more transparent and rigorous discussions about it?

Is this a public health emergency that warrants the $1+ billion a year the U.S. is spending on it? Or are we fighting a war that's unjustified, unjust, and impossible to win?

> "The stigma once rightly associated with obesity is disappearing as quickly as fat is accumulating."

Society Should Stigmatize Being Obese

Christopher Freind

In the following viewpoint, Christopher Freind asserts that obese people should be shamed into losing weight. In his opinion, they are obese only because they eat too much, and since telling them that obesity can cause serious health problems does not work, they should be made to feel that it is socially unacceptable. He believes this would be the best, and in fact the only, way of reducing the costs associated with obesity that society must subsidize. Freind is an independent columnist, television commentator, and investigative reporter who operates his own news bureau, Freindly Fire Zone Media.

As you read, consider the following questions:

1. What kind of advertising does Freind think would have a positive effect on the problem of obesity?

2. What evidence does Freind present to support his belief that shaming people works?

3. What examples does Freind give of ways in which the cost of accommodating obese people raises prices for everyone?

Several years ago, one of the best-loved theme parks in the world shut down a classic ride so it could make some adjustments: People had become so obese that the ride's boats were scraping the bottom.

How would obese patrons feel if, in front of hundreds, they were required to stand in a different queue—one simply marked "Obese Riders Here"? And instead of meeting just a height requirement, theme park guests were also forced to meet a "width" criteria.

Or when boarding an airplane, fat people would be called separately so they could sit in extra-wide seats, for which they pay double?

And what if stadiums had a section of reinforced double-wide seats where obese folks were required to sit?

Unfortunately, our country doesn't go for such options, which is truly a shame.

And that's precisely the problem. *There is no shame.*

In genuflecting to political correctness, America shuns shame. It has become a nation so afraid to offend that it turns a blind eye to its *biggest* problems, such as obesity. And that problem is burgeoning. Two-thirds of Americans are overweight or obese, and a staggering percentage of our children—our future—are growing up (and out) with little regard for how this epidemic will impact them. In this regard, some medical experts have predicted that our children may be the first generation to have a shorter life expectancy than their parents. For many, they are the product of their environment, where parents (many obese themselves) and society as a whole have sent the message that being fat is no "big" deal. The stigma once rightly associated with obesity is disappearing as quickly as fat is accumulating.

So how do we get to the bottom of this problem? For starters, shame. Because no matter what else is attempted, if shame is not the cornerstone of the solution, the situation will never improve.

Effective Campaigns

Two fantastic and courageous examples of how shame is being effectively utilized are occurring in Georgia and Minnesota. In Atlanta, an extensive advertising campaign "Stop Sugarcoating It," sponsored by Children's Healthcare [of Atlanta], targets childhood obesity. Taglines under obese children include "Warning . . . It's hard to be a little girl if you're not"; "Being fat takes the fun out of being a kid"; and "Big Bones Didn't Make Me This Way . . . Big Meals Did." There was also a YouTube ad with a sad girl saying, "I don't like going to school, because all the other kids pick on me. It hurts my feelings."

Blue Cross and Blue Shield of Minnesota has launched a similar campaign, targeting overweight parents whose behavior is often mimicked by their children. One ad shows two chubby boys arguing about whose dad can eat more—a discussion overheard by a father as he approaches their table with a heaping tray of fast food. Another shows an obese woman filling her shopping cart with junk food, only to notice that her obese daughter is doing the exact same thing with a smaller cart.

Both campaigns use shame correctly. Without being mean-spirited or over the top, they prod people to acknowledge, and change, their unhealthy behavior. Not surprisingly, though, both have something else in common: They've received significant criticism from the waistline-challenged community. Their biggest beef? It's not education, but shaming, which, of course is "bullying."

They simply don't get it.

Shaming isn't the total panacea, but it *must* be an integral part of the solution. There's no better example of how shame can change perceptions than smoking, which was once considered cool but is now viewed with utter disdain. Sure, cigarettes are expensive, but that's not why smoking is down. It's because society made a conscious effort to shame smokers. Try lighting up in a bar with coworkers, and you receive dagger-like stares. Do it outside, and people immediately move away, because smoking is regarded as disgusting, and therefore, the smoker must be, too.

Smoking kills, and we have no problem pointing out *that* as a deterrent. Yet so does obesity, and we still hesitate to mention it. Just as non-smokers are picking up the tab for the massive medical costs related to smoking, non-overweight people are subsidizing the obese since it is "discriminatory" to charge differently for health care (though a section of the [Patient Protection and] Affordable Care Act would change that).

Shameful Situations

But shaming is now taboo, and no one is ever at fault or accountable for his actions. Consider:

- It used to be, when a student received a detention, they weren't just shamed in front of their classmates. They knew they had to tell their parents, which would invariably trigger another punishment.

- Contrast that to the reaction this week to a New Jersey principal's letter to parents about pictures of their underage children on Facebook holding alcohol bottles. Instead of thanking the principal for bringing that situation to their attention, a number of parents ripped him.

- Airlines have attempted to charge double for obese passengers whose girth extends beyond the armrests. While this is clearly common sense, since not doing so penal-

Obesity Should Be Made Socially Unacceptable

It will be . . . necessary to find ways to bring strong social pressure to bear on individuals, going beyond anodyne education and low-key exhortation. It will be imperative, first, to persuade them that they ought to want a good diet and exercise for themselves and for their neighbor and, second, that excessive weight and outright obesity are not socially acceptable any longer. They need as well to be mobilized as citizens to support a more invasive role for government. Obesity is in great part a reflection of the kind or culture we have, one that is permissive about how people take care of their bodies and accepts many if not most of the features of our society that contribute to the problem. There has to be a popular uprising when so many aspects of our common lives, individually and institutionally, must be changed more or less simultaneously. Safe and slow incrementalism that strives never to stigmatize obesity has not and cannot do the necessary work.

Daniel Callahan, "Obesity: Chasing an Elusive Epidemic,"
Hastings Center Report, *January–February 2013.*

izes paying passengers of normal weight, such policies are met with scorn and even lawsuits by those lobbying for obesity without consequence.

• And since it would be considered "discriminatory" to have an obese-only section in stadiums, seats are being made wider to accommodate overly plump posteriors. And when seats are wider, there are fewer of them. Who pays? You do. The same way that the non-obese eat the cost of new toilets that must be installed with ground supports, as the standard wall-mounted com-modes can no longer bear the weight of America's fat brigade.

We have coddled ourselves so much that we have shamed using shame. As a result, people have become clueless to their appearance. Sure, what's under the skin matters, and no one should feel that obese people are bad, but what's on the out-side counts, too. Or at least it should. But go to any beach, and count how many linebacker-sized women are showcasing themselves in bikinis. Ditto for men whose guts reach the next block. Since they all have mirrors, one can only assume that shame is simply not a part of their lives.

Should we have scarlet letters for the obese? Of course not, since there is no problem identifying them. But we should employ shame to shed light on an issue that affects us all, in the same way that some judges order drunk drivers to place "Convicted DUI" bumper stickers on their cars.

And speaking of cars, how shameful is it that overweight people are not just guzzling food, but fuel? A recent report calculated that one billion gallons of gasoline are wasted every year (one percent of the nation's total) just to haul Americans' extra pounds. And given that the average American weighs 24 more pounds than in 1960, airlines are using roughly 175 mil-lion more gallons of jet fuel *per year* just to accommodate the overweight. That's downright shameful.

And if not shame, then what? Do we tax fast food? Soda? Candy? Do we regulate portion size? No. Not only are such ideas preposterous and unenforceable, but they are tactics, not strategy. It's time to tip the scales against obesity and *solve the problem.*

Otherwise, we will soon find out that the "elephant in the room" isn't a pachyderm at all.

It's an average American.

| *"Telling fat people they ought to be thin is about as helpful as telling gay people they should be straight."*

Stigmatizing Obese People Is Comparable to Stigmatizing Gay Individuals

Paul Campos

In the following viewpoint, Paul Campos points out the past and present parallels between society's attitude toward gay people and its attitude toward obese people. Around the turn of the twentieth century, he says, both homosexuality and obesity came to be viewed as diseases rather than mere deviations from social norms, and doctors attempted to cure them. In the latter part of the century, activists challenged the idea that these are pathological medical conditions; however, whereas gay rights advocates have been successful in that respect, fat rights advocates have so far been unable to overcome cultural prejudices. Campos is a professor of law at the University of Colorado, Boulder. He is a widely published journalist and the author of The Obesity Myth: Why America's Obsession with Weight Is Hazardous to Your Health.

Paul Campos, "Anti-Obesity: The New Homophobia?," *Salon*, August 28, 2012. This article first appeared in Salon.com, at http://www.Salon.com. An online version remains in the Salon archives. Reprinted with permission.

As you read, consider the following questions:

1. According to Campos, what do the gay rights movement and the fat rights movement have in common?

2. What does Campos consider the most striking parallel between attempts to turn gay people into straight people and efforts to turn fat people into thin people?

3. In Campos's opinion, what is the underlying reason why society pathologized both homosexuality and obesity?

This week [in August 2012] a Boston-area doctor revealed she will no longer accept patients who weigh more than 200 pounds, because fat people are dangerous deviants who should go to "obesity centers" to get treated for their "disease." Earlier this summer, a gay man accused a New Jersey doctor of refusing to treat him because, allegedly, she attributed his need for medical care to "going against God's will."

"Homosexuality" and "obesity" are both diseases invented around the turn of the previous century. Prior to that time, being sexually attracted to someone of the same gender or having a larger than average body were, to the extent they were thought of as social problems, considered moral rather than medical issues: That is, they were seen as manifestations of morally problematic appetites, rather than disease states.

The same medical establishment that pathologized same-sex sexual attraction and larger bodies also offered up cures for these newly discovered diseases. Those who deviated from social norms were assured that, with the help of medical science, homosexuals and the obese could become "normal," that is, heterosexual and thin.

In the latter half of the 20th century these frames were challenged by gay rights and fat rights advocates. Within these movements, the words "gay" and "fat" had similar purposes. They were intended to de-pathologize what medicine called "homosexuality" and "obesity," by asserting that different sexual orientations and body sizes were both inevitable and largely unalterable, and that being gay or fat was not a disease.

Over the past few decades, gay rights activists have had great success challenging what 50 years ago was the standard medical view that "homosexuality" constituted a disease. By contrast, fat rights activists still deal with a public health establishment that continues to reflect and replicate profound cultural prejudices when it advocates ineffective cures for an imaginary illness.

The extent to which the construction of "obesity" as a social problem has paralleled the history of the medical establishment's construction of the concept of "homosexuality" can be seen by comparing the cures put forth for these purported diseases.

To a remarkable degree, attempts to cure obesity resemble attempted cures for homosexuality, with the key difference being that while our public health authorities have come to denounce the latter as ineffective, unnecessary and ultimately harmful, they continue to employ the most extreme rhetoric in regard to the former. For example, the goal of Michelle Obama's Let's Move! campaign is no less than to "end childhood obesity within a generation," that is, to create an America with no fat children in it.

Parallels Between Homosexuality and Obesity

Consider the many parallels between the treatments advocated by those who claim being gay is a disease, and those being pushed by our public health establishment to "cure" fat children and adults of their supposedly pathological state.

The advocates of so-called conversion or reparative therapy believe that "homosexuality" is a curable condition, and that a key to successful treatment is that patients must want to be cured, which is to say they consider same-sex sexual orientation volitional. These beliefs mirror precisely those of the obesity establishment, which claims to offer the means by which fat people who want to choose to stop being fat can successfully make that choice.

Those who seek to cure homosexuality and obesity have tended to react to the failure of their attempts by demanding ever more radical interventions. For example, in the 1950s Edmund Bergler, the most influential psychoanalytical theorist of homosexuality of his era, bullied and berated his clients, violated patient confidentiality and renounced his earlier, more tolerant attitude toward gay people as a form of enabling. Meanwhile, earlier this year a Harvard biology professor declared in a public lecture that Mrs. Obama's call for voluntary lifestyle changes on the part of the obese constituted an insufficient response to the supposed public health calamity overwhelming the nation, and that the government should legally require fat people to exercise.

Anti-gay and anti-fat zealots both try to build support for their initiatives by defining success down: Advocates of conversion therapy claim their treatments "work" if patients are able to achieve sexual potency in a heterosexual encounter, or are able to avoid same-sex sexual contact for a period of weeks or months, even if they experience no lessening of desire for such contact. This lowering of the bar for what constitutes a cure is mirrored by public health authorities touting short-term weight loss or small losses of body weight as evidence for the success of anti-obesity programs.

Indeed, the most striking parallel between attempts to turn gay people into straight people and efforts to turn fat people into thin people is that both almost invariably fail. The long-term success rate of such attempts is extremely low. When it comes to the various forms of conversion therapy, the medical establishment now acknowledges this. This acknowledgment, in turn, has helped medical authorities recognize that it does not make sense to label "homosexuality" a

The Right to Be Fat

The central rationale behind the right to be fat is that sending a direct or an indirect message to a fat person that he or she needs to lose weight in order to gain access to various social goods, such as equal opportunity, dignity, and autonomy, is no less intrusive than telling a legal subject how to think, what to believe, or what to say. . . .

One need not justify the usefulness or truthfulness of one's speech before one utters it. . . . Legal subjects are . . . allowed to produce the most bizarre, nonsensical, and even, to some extent, harmful speech. In the end, according to contemporary American constitutional law, individual freedom to think and speak is, in most instances, more important than the potential costs and damages of speech. . . .

Limiting body weight is analogous to limiting speech in that both can be potentially intrusive. . . . Weight should not be assessed merely through its alleged social cost, but respected as a domain of self that is as intimate to individual privacy and autonomy as faith, conscience, thought, or speech. . . . Even readers who are convinced that being fat without making efforts to lose weight is a bad lifestyle choice should endorse the right to be fat. They should view it as the right to make one's own mistakes in one's own way. This is how we think of ill-informed speech. As mistaken as it may be, it should still be protected, because the damage of limiting it and interfering with it would outweigh the benefits of such constraints.

Yofi Tirosh, "The Right to Be Fat,"
Yale Journal of Health Policy, Law, and Ethics,
vol. 12, no. 2, 2012.

disease, and that therapy for same-sex sexual attraction is both unnecessary and more likely to do harm than good.

But when it comes to fat, the fear and disgust elicited in this culture by fat bodies (reminiscent of the reactions elicited traditionally by same-sex sexual relations) prevents the public health establishment from recognizing that the various "cures" it advocates for "obesity" have been demonstrated again and again to be every bit as ineffective as conversion therapy has been shown to be for "homosexuality."

Why Homosexuality and Obesity Were Labeled "Curable"

The pathologizing of gay and fat bodies springs ultimately from the same cultural source: the desire to ground moral and aesthetic disapproval in the supposedly objective discourse of science and health. It is true that fat people are at a higher risk for certain diseases (although the extent to which higher weight correlates with increased mortality and morbidity is greatly exaggerated). But trying to, for example, lessen the prevalence of diabetes by eliminating "obesity" makes no more sense than trying to lessen the prevalence of HIV infection by eliminating "homosexuality."

The extent to which either one's sexual orientation or one's weight are chosen states is minimal. With rare exceptions, people cannot intentionally alter either their sexual orientation or their weight in a long-term way. Given all this, to label same-sex orientation or higher than average body weight as diseases stigmatizes those who are so labeled to no purpose, other than to express disapproval of deviance from social norms to which the stigmatized cannot adhere.

Telling fat people they ought to be thin is about as helpful as telling gay people they should be straight. It took many decades for the medical establishment to recognize that its "cures" for "homosexuality" did far more damage than the imaginary disease to which they were addressed, and that the biggest favor it could do for gay people was to stop harassing them. Fat people are still waiting for the same favor.

Periodical and Internet Sources Bibliography

The following articles have been selected to supplement the diverse views presented in this chapter.

Sharon Begley	"Insight: America's Hatred of Fat Hurts Obesity Fight," *Reuters*, May 11, 2012.
Daniel Callahan	"Obesity: Chasing an Elusive Epidemic," *Hastings Center Report*, January–February 2013.
Felicity Cloake	"Our Big Fat Fear," *New Statesman*, May 23, 2013.
Geoffrey Cowley	"Let's Move (Faster) on Childhood Obesity," *MSNBC*, January 28, 2013.
Anthony T. DeBenedet	"Is the Fight Against Childhood Obesity Creating Eating Disorders?," *Time*, February 21, 2012.
Monica Dux	"Too Fat, Too Thin: A Sickening Debate for Our Teenagers," *Sydney Morning Herald*, October 7, 2012.
Thomas A. Farley	"The Role of Government in Preventing Excess Calorie Consumption: The Example of New York City," *Journal of the American Medical Association*, September 19, 2012.
James Huffman	"Let Them Drink Big Sodas," *Defining Ideas*, April 3, 2013.
Brooke Kantor and Hannah Borowsky	"The Obesity–Eating Disorder Paradox," *Harvard Political Review*, April 1, 2012.
Yofi Tirosh	"The Right to Be Fat," *Yale Journal of Health Policy, Law, and Ethics*, vol. 12, no. 2, 2012.

What Is Causing the Rise in Obesity?

Chapter Preface

According to the prevailing view, the reason for the rise in obesity during the past few decades is that people have been eating more and getting less exercise than they did in the past. Until recently, this explanation was not challenged. Now, however, some experts have begun to believe that this view is a simplistic explanation that cannot account for the increasing percentage of obese people. There are a number of reasons for their skepticism, but one of the strongest and most compelling is the fact that animals, too, have been getting fatter. "Could our inability to explain animal obesity with behavior be a warning sign?," wrote Harvard professor Sendhil Mullainathan in a November 9, 2013, article in the *New York Times*. "Perhaps we are also overlooking biological drivers for human obesity."

If it were just a matter of overweight pets, animal weight gain would be easy to understand. Many pets are overfed, and many are less active than in the past because fewer of them are allowed to run free. The rise in animal obesity, however, is not limited to dogs, cats, and zoo animals, to which similar considerations apply. It has also been observed both in laboratory animals, which have a strictly controlled diet, and in some wild animals. In a University of Alabama study reported in 2010, researchers examined more than twenty thousand samples from eight species—several separate populations of each—and found that the average weight of all of them had increased. Besides dogs and cats, this included chimpanzees, macaques, vervets, marmosets, laboratory rats and mice, and feral rats.

Other studies have shown an increase in obesity among species as diverse as pasture-fed horses and wild mountain marmots. Various explanations have been offered for this trend, some of which are applicable only to specific animal situations. However, they do not apply to all of them, leading many scientists to believe that something not unique to humans is at least partially responsible for the rise in obesity. This is important to investigate because, biologically, people are animals, and it is unlikely that they would be unaffected by whatever is affecting other animal species.

The researcher who led the University of Alabama study, David Allison, wrote, "The consistency of these findings among animals living in varying environments suggests the intriguing possibility that the aetiology [origin] of increasing body weight may involve several as-of-yet unidentified and/or poorly understood factors." Such factors, if discovered, would explain why the average weight of so many animal species, including humans, has been rising.

Various possibilities have been suggested. One that has gained wide attention is the presence of toxic chemicals in the environment, as there is evidence that they may affect both human and animal metabolism. Another is the impact of antibiotics, traces of which may be present in the meat humans eat and which can alter the beneficial bacteria in the digestive system. There has also been research into whether a virus may be involved. Some researchers believe that even climate change may be affecting weight. While it is conceivable that obesity may increase in different species for different reasons, the odds are against it; therefore, scientists are beginning to look for some common cause.

If there is such a cause, it is vital that it be found. Just as the study of animal biology has been invaluable to medical science in other areas, it may provide key information about the causes of variation in humans' weight. As Allison concluded, "Our findings in other animals add to the increasing evidence that other potential risk factors . . . should be incorporated into public health research and environmental medicine."

The viewpoints in this chapter discuss some of the factors that may be contributing to the rise in obesity.

"*Researchers reporting at the European Congress on Obesity in Amsterdam found that excess food intake alone explains the obesity epidemic.*"

The Rise in Obesity Is Due Mainly to Overeating

Kristina Fiore

In the following viewpoint, Kristina Fiore reports on a study that found overeating to be the main cause of the rise in obesity. Researchers compared actual weight gain among the study's subjects with the weight gain that could be expected from food supply consumption and found that it was no greater. Fiore points out that these findings were consistent with data showing that food consumption has increased since the 1970s, but exercise levels have barely changed. In the opinion of the study's leader, public health policy should be focused on encouraging people to eat less. Fiore is a staff writer for the website MedPage Today.

As you read, consider the following questions:

1. What kinds of data did researchers in the study reported by Fiore use to determine that excess food intake is the cause of the obesity epidemic?

2. How did the leader of the study explain the fact that adults in the study gained less weight than was predicted?

3. Why did researchers at the University of California, San Francisco, suspect that exercise plays only a minor role in obesity?

The rise of obesity in the U.S. is almost entirely due to overeating, not declining physical activity levels, researchers have found.

Using equations based on biological, epidemiological, and food supply factors, researchers reporting at the European Congress on Obesity in Amsterdam found that excess food intake alone explains the obesity epidemic.

"Weight gain in the American population seems to be virtually all explained by eating more calories," said Boyd Swinburn, M.D., of Deakin University in Australia, lead author of the study. "It appears that changes in physical activity played a minimal role."

There has been much debate about how much of the obesity epidemic is due to overeating and how much by reductions in physical activity.

To sort out the contributions of each factor, the researchers derived equations relating stable weight to energy flux by combining metabolic relationships, the laws of thermodynamics, epidemiological data, and agricultural data.

They looked at 1,399 adults and 963 children to determine how many calories their bodies burn under normal living conditions. Then they figured out how much adults need to eat in order to maintain a stable weight—and how much children must eat to maintain a normal growth curve.

Using national food supply data from the 1970s and the early 2000s, the researchers worked out how much Americans were actually eating. NHANES [National Health and Nutri-

Increasing Physical Activity May Have Little Impact on Obesity

Our results showed an increase in the prevalence of sufficient physical activity from 2001 to 2009. Levels were generally higher in men than in women, but increases were greater in women than men.... This increase in level of activity was matched by an increase in obesity in almost all [US] counties during the same time period. There was a low correlation between level of physical activity and obesity in US counties. From 2001 to 2009, controlling for changes in poverty, unemployment, number of doctors per 100,000 population, percent rural, and baseline levels of obesity, for every 1 percentage point increase in physical activity prevalence, obesity prevalence was 0.11 percentage points lower.

Our study showed that increased physical activity alone has a small impact on obesity prevalence at the county level in the US. Indeed, the rise in physical activity levels will have a positive independent impact on the health of Americans as it will reduce the burden of cardiovascular diseases and diabetes. Other changes such as reduction in caloric intake are likely needed to curb the obesity epidemic and its burden.

Laura Dwyer-Lindgren et al.,
"Prevalence of Physical Activity and Obesity
in US Counties, 2001–2011: A Road Map for Action,"
Population Health Metrics, *vol. 11, no. 7, 2013.*

tion Examination Survey] data on population weight during that time period was used to determine actual weight gain. From this information, the researchers could predict how much weight they would expect Americans to gain over the 30-year period had food intake been the only influence.

Food Intake Could Explain the Actual Weight Gain

In children, the predicted weight increase matched the actual increase (4.0 kg), suggesting that increases in energy intake alone could have explained it.

Adults actually gained less than the predicted increase—8.6 kg versus 10.8 kg—which suggests that "excess food intake still explains the weight gain, but there may have been increases in physical activity over the 30 years that have blunted what would otherwise have been a higher weight gain," Dr. Swinburn said. He said the findings support epidemiological data showing that physical activity levels have barely changed, whereas total energy intake has increased.

Dr. Swinburn added that physical activity is still an important part of reducing obesity, and should still be touted for its many other benefits. However, he said, public health policy should be shifted more toward encouraging patients to eat less.

"We have long suspected that the decrease in physical activity seen during the past 30 years is playing a minor role in the change in body weight," said Robert Lustig, M.D., an obesity researcher at the University of California, San Francisco. "This was inferred by the fact that virtually all studies of increased exercise in obesity did not translate into weight loss."

He added that exercise plays an essential role in the obesity epidemic, not because it reduces excess weight, but because it improves health. Twenty minutes of jogging, for example, burns the equivalent of a chocolate chip cookie, he said. Thus, Americans "need a complete overhaul of our diet if we are to solve the obesity epidemic," Dr. Lustig said.

Others took a more nuanced view of the findings. Hugh S. Taylor, M.D., an endocrinologist at Yale, said there are other possible explanations for the obesity epidemic beyond the two put forward in the study.

The researchers "should also consider the effect of reduced exercise in children that may predispose to obesity later in life," Dr. Taylor said. "And there is now growing evidence that chemicals in the environment which disrupt the endocrine system—such as bisphenol A or BPA—also can lead to weight gain."

He said that diet as the major determinate of obesity is "not surprising," but "we cannot overlook the other determinates of obesity, namely exercise and hormones. These may impact on our drive to eat and when we feel full."

> "Reduction in occupational energy expenditure accounts for a large portion of the observed increase in mean U.S. weight over the last 5 decades."

The Rise in Obesity Is Due Mainly to Physical Inactivity

Timothy S. Church et al.

In the following viewpoint, Timothy S. Church and his coauthors explain that during the past fifty years there has been a significant decrease in the number of people employed in occupations requiring physical activity and a corresponding increase in those doing sedentary work, and that this accounts for a large part of the increase in average weight. Because of the reduction in job-related physical activity, they say, public health authorities should promote physical activity outside work hours, as most people do not get enough exercise. Church is a professor at the Pennington Biomedical Research Center of Louisiana State University.

As you read, consider the following questions:

1. What changes in physical activity do the authors say they omitted from their study?

Timothy S. Church et al., "Trends Over 5 Decades in U.S. Occupation-Related Physical Activity and Their Association with Obesity," *PLoS One*, May 25, 2011. Licensed under CC by 3.0. Reproduced by permission.

2. According to the authors, how much leisure-time physical activity would compensate for the reduction in work-related activity?

3. According to the viewpoint, why are previous studies showing that food consumption can account for the population's weight gain not valid?

Over the last 50 years in the U.S. there has been a progressive decrease in the percent of individuals employed in goods producing and agriculture occupations whereas there has been an increase in the percent of individuals employed in service occupations. This has resulted in a shift away from occupations that require moderate-intensity physical activity to occupations that are largely composed of sitting and sedentary behavior. In the early 1960s almost half of private industry occupations in the U.S. required at least moderate-intensity physical activity and now less than 20% demand this level of activity. We estimate that daily occupation-related energy expenditure has decreased by more than 100 calories in both women and men, and further, this reduction in occupational energy expenditure accounts for a large portion of the observed increase in mean U.S. weight over the last 5 decades.

Examining secular changes in total daily physical activity is a complex endeavor. Two examples include the observation that time spent in recreational activities has increased but so has time spent watching TV. At the same time, time spent on household work has greatly decreased in women but slightly increased in men. Dissecting the relative importance of each of these activities of daily living on body weight is challenging. Here we chose to focus on occupation-related energy expenditure because time spent at work represents the largest segment of waking hours for most people in the age range we studied. It is important to note that we examined the prevalence of different occupations, not absolute number of jobs in a given occupation. This is important because the workforce is not a static population and over the last 50 years the prevalence of Americans in the labor force has increased from approximately 40% to 50%. One of the driving forces behind the increased prevalence of working Americans is the increase of women in the workforce. In 1970 43% percent of women were in the labor force and by 2007 this increased to 60% of women. This fact may also explain why occupation-related energy expenditure estimated a higher mean weight during the years of 1971 to 1994 but closely matched the mean weight of women from NHANES [National Health and Nutrition Examination Survey] during the period of 1999–2002.

The Need for Active Lifestyles Outside Work

Given that it is unlikely that there will be a return to occupations that demand moderate levels of physical activity, our findings provide further strong evidence of the public health importance of promoting physically active lifestyles outside of the workday. Our estimation of a reduction of more than 100 calories per day in occupation-related energy expenditure over the last 50 years would have been adequately compensated for by meeting the 2008 federal physical activity recommendations of 150 minutes per week of moderate-intensity activity or 75 minutes per week of vigorous-intensity activity. While it is often noted that the prevalence of Americans who achieve this recommendation has been constant over recent decades, the fact remains that based on self-report data only 1 in 4 Americans achieve this level. It is important to note that when physical activity is assessed with accelerometers the number of Americans that achieve the physical activity recommendations falls to 1 in 20. Thus since energy expenditure has largely been removed from the workplace the relative importance of leisure-time physical activity has increased and should be a major focus of public health interventions and research.

Based on estimated calorie consumption from food production and food disappearance (food waste) estimates, previous reports have concluded that increased caloric consumption could account for most, if not all, of the weight gained at a population level in the U.S. Nonetheless, a recently validated differential equation model was used to identify a conservative lower bound for the amount of food waste in the U.S. This analysis determined that prior estimates of national food waste were grossly underestimated; indicating that the national average caloric intake was lower than previously estimated. These results and the results of the present study indicate that changes in caloric intake cannot solely account for the observed trends in national weight gain.

Limitations of the Study

Our analysis has strengths and weaknesses that deserve mention. A major strength of this analysis is that for both the U.S. obesity and occupation data we used nationally representative databases. Further, we used a previously published and well-recognized classification system to assign physical activity intensity levels to each occupation category thus minimizing the possibility of misclassifying occupation-related physical activity intensity. However, we used the same physical activity classifications across the 5 decades examined and in doing so we did not take into account changes in technology that have reduced physical labor. While technological advances have greatly reduced the physical labor associated with most manufacturing operations this phenomenon would drive our results towards the null and thus we may be underestimating the true loss of moderate-intensity occupations in the workforce. Our analysis was focused on type of occupation, and there are many aspects of occupation-related daily energy expenditure we did not examine such as mode of travel to work, total sitting time and stair usage. Another weakness of our analysis is that not all agricultural or goods-producing occupations are associated with higher levels of physical activity and conversely some service-related occupations are associated with higher levels of physical activity. However, there are no adequate data to examine this level of detail and we were very conservative in assigning MET [metabolic equivalents] values in order to minimize the effect of such misclassification within occupation types.

Over the last 50 years in the U.S. there has been a progressive decrease in the percent of individuals employed in occupations that require moderate-intensity physical activity. We estimate that daily occupation-related energy expenditure has decreased by more than 100 calories, and this reduction in energy expenditure accounts for a significant portion of the increase in mean U.S. body weight for women and men over the last 5 decades.

> *"Returning to a diet of simple home-cooked food, made from minimally refined ingredients, would probably stop the obesity epidemic in its tracks."*

Seduced by Food: Obesity and the Human Brain

Stephan J. Guyenet

In the following viewpoint, Stephan J. Guyenet explains what science has learned about how commercially prepared foods contribute to obesity. The human brain is affected by hormones that regulate appetite and the body's use of calories, he says; restriction of calorie intake causes the brain to signal that it is starving even if the body is fat, and vice versa. Especially palatable food disrupts this system, and the American diet has, over time, become increasingly palatable because food manufacturers design it to be. This, Guyenet states, is why junk food is so harmful to health. In his opinion, people should go back to a less palatable diet. Guyenet is an obesity researcher at the University of Washington.

As you read, consider the following questions:

1. What does the hormone leptin do, according to Guyenet's explanation?

2. As stated by Guyenet, what kind of diet is especially fattening to rats?

3. According to Guyenet, why do opposite kinds of diets, such as low-fat vs. low-carbohydrate ones, both result in weight loss?

In 1960–1962, the US government collected height and weight measurements from thousands of US citizens. Using these numbers, they estimated that the prevalence of obesity among US adults at the time was 13 percent. Fast-forward to the year 2007–2008, and in the same demographic group, the prevalence of obesity was 34 percent (1). Most of this increase has occurred since 1980, when obesity rates have more than doubled among US adults, and extreme obesity has more than tripled. Welcome to the 'obesity epidemic'. Today, more than one-third of US adults are considered obese, an additional third are overweight, and largely as a consequence, each child born today has an estimated one in three risk of developing diabetes in his or her lifetime.

Since the obesity epidemic is a serious threat to public health and well-being, scientists have made it a research priority, and our understanding of its causes and consequences is rapidly expanding. Obesity can be the result of many interacting factors, including genetic makeup, developmental factors, physical inactivity, stress, insufficient sleep, social factors and smoking cessation. But dietary changes are clearly an outsized contributor. The obesity epidemic has closely paralleled a large (approximately 20%) increase in per capita calorie intake, and according to the best available mathematical models, this increase can single-handedly account for the increase in body fatness over the last 30 years (2, 3).

Calories are interesting, but let's delve deeper. We didn't just wake up one day and decide to eat more—something is driving our increased food intake. But what? Research accumulated over the last two centuries has revealed that the answer lies in the intricacies of the human brain.

The Human Brain and Obesity

In 1840, a German doctor named B. Mohr made a critical observation while performing autopsies on obese subjects: some of them had damage in a part of the brain called the hypothalamus (B. Mohr. Wschr Heilkd, 6:565–574. 1840). Over the ensuing century and a half, researchers gradually uncovered a network of circuits in the hypothalamus dedicated to maintaining the stability (homeostasis) of body fat stores, by regulating food intake, energy expenditure, and the deposition of energy in fat tissue. This research culminated in the discovery of an extraordinary hormone called leptin in 1994. Produced by fat tissue in proportion to its mass, leptin enters the circulation and acts in the hypothalamus to regulate body fat stores. If you consistently restrict food intake, fat mass declines and so does leptin, and this signals the hypothalamus to stimulate hunger and make the body use calories more efficiently, in an attempt to regain lost body fat (4). Conversely, if you consistently overeat, the increase in fat mass and leptin suppresses appetite and increases calorie use until body fat stores have declined back to baseline (5, 6). Leptin and a few other hormones are part of a negative feedback loop that acts unconsciously to keep fat mass in a specific range, sort of like a thermostat does for temperature (7, 8). This is called the 'energy homeostasis system'.

So if we have this built-in system to regulate body fatness, how does anyone become obese? Some researchers believe the energy homeostasis system defends against fat loss more effectively than fat gain. However, most obese people regulate their body fat just fine, but their brains 'defend' it at a higher level than a lean person. Going back to the thermostat analogy, in obese people it's like the 'temperature' has been gradually turned up. That's why it's so hard to maintain weight loss—

when body fat stores decline, the brain thinks it's starving even if fat mass remains high—and it acts to regain the lost fat. If we want to understand how to prevent and treat obesity, first we have to understand why obese people defend a higher level of fat mass than lean people.

The Most Fattening Diet in the World

To understand how this happens, let's turn to animal research. Although rodents aren't humans, they resemble us in many ways. Just like humans, rodents evolved to regulate body fat around an 'optimal' level to maximize survival and reproduction, and their systems for doing this are very similar to ours. Rodents also offer us the ability to control variables much more tightly than in human research. There are many ways to make a rat obese, but some are more effective than others. High-fat pelleted diets, composed of refined ingredients, are most common because they're reliably fattening and their composition can be tightly controlled. But another diet, seldom used, is the most fattening of all: the 'cafeteria diet'. This diet has a lot to tell us about the expanding American waistline.

First described in 1976 by Anthony Sclafani, the cafeteria diet is basically a rat-sized buffet of human junk food, in addition to regular rat chow (9). The menu for a recent cafeteria diet study included such delectable items as Froot Loops, mini hot dogs, peanut butter cookies, Cheez-Its, Cocoa Puffs, nacho cheese Doritos, cake, and BBQ pork rinds (10). These are what's known in the business as 'palatable', or pleasurable to the taste. On this regimen, rats ignored their regular chow, ate junk food to excess and gained fat at an extraordinary rate, far outpacing two comparison groups fed high-fat or high-sugar pelleted diets. Yes, human junk food happens to be the most effective way to overwhelm the body fat homeostasis system in rats, and neither fat nor sugar alone is able to fully explain why it's so fattening. Importantly, over time, rats become highly motivated to obtain this diet—so motivated they'll voluntarily endure extreme cold temperatures and electric shocks to obtain it, even when regular bland rodent pellets are freely available (11, 12).

The cafeteria diet is an exaggerated version of an unhealthy human diet, and not many people eat quite that poorly. However, have a look at the top six calorie sources in the current US diet, in order of calorie contribution: grain-based desserts (cake, cookies, etc.), yeast breads, chicken-based dishes, sweetened beverages, pizza and alcoholic beverages (13). Our eating habits aren't as different from the cafeteria diet as we might like to believe.

In 1992, Eric Ravussin and collaborators tried to repeat the rodent experiment in humans. They gave volunteers unlimited access to a large variety of palatable energy-dense foods, in a setting where the researchers could monitor exactly what was eaten. Over the course of the next week, the volunteers more than doubled their usual calorie intake, gaining an average of five pounds (14). Further studies showed a similar effect (15, 16). Just as in rats, exposing humans to a large variety of palatable energy-dense foods causes an increase in food intake and rapid fat gain. To explain this, we need to bring our attention back to the brain.

My Neurons Made Me Fat

To understand why junk food causes fat gain in rats and humans, we have to explore two other circuits in the brain, beginning with the reward system. The reward system acts to gauge the desirability of food (among other stimuli) and reinforce and motivate behaviors that favor the acquisition of desirable food. For example, if you eat a strong cheese for the first time, maybe it won't taste very good to you. As it's digested, your reward system gets wind that it's full of calories, and the next few times you eat it, it tastes better and better until you like the flavor (17, 18). This is called an acquired

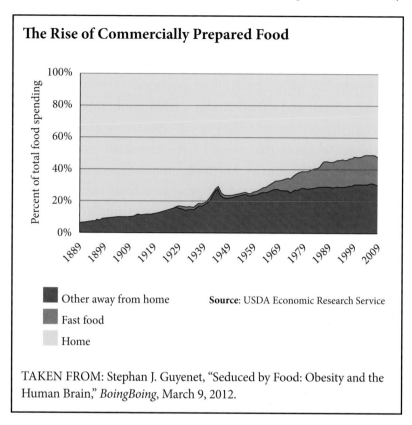

The Rise of Commercially Prepared Food

■ Other away from home   **Source**: USDA Economic Research Service
■ Fast food
□ Home

TAKEN FROM: Stephan J. Guyenet, "Seduced by Food: Obesity and the Human Brain," *BoingBoing*, March 9, 2012.

taste, and the reward system is what does the acquiring, motivating you to obtain a food it has deemed safe and desirable. This is the same process that allows children to learn to like vegetables—which are low-calorie, often bitter foods that are initially unpalatable—if they're repeatedly paired with fat, salt or some other desirable quality. The reward system does the same thing with foods/beverages that contain drugs, such as coffee and beer, gradually making bitter fluids palatable and then delicious.

Eventually, you may go out of your way to purchase the cheese or beer at the grocery store, and maybe you'll consume cheese or beer even if you aren't hungry or thirsty, simply because you like it. This is an example of the reward system reinforcing and motivating behaviors related to foods it considers desirable. What does the reward system consider desirable? Calorie density, fat, starch, sugar, salt, free glutamate (umami), certain textures (easily chewed, soft or crunchy, solid fat), certain flavors, an absence of bitterness, food variety, and drugs such as alcohol and caffeine. Our brains are highly attuned to these qualities because they're all elements of nutritious, calorie-dense foods that would have sustained our ancestors in a natural environment, but today, the exaggerated combinations of these qualities used by processed food manufacturers, chefs and sometimes even home cooks overstimulate our natural reward pathways (19). Commercial foods are professionally designed to maximize reward, because reward is precisely what keeps you coming back for more. Processed junk foods such as ice cream, fast food, sweetened soda, cookies, cake, candy, pizza and deep-fried foods are all archetypal hyper-rewarding foods.

Palatability is a related concept—it's determined in part by inborn preferences (e.g., a taste for sugar and energy dense foods), and in part by the reward system (acquired tastes). Palatability is governed by the hedonic system in the brain, which is closely integrated with the reward system. Imagine yourself sitting at the dinner table, stuffed after a large meal. Then the cake and ice cream appear, and suddenly you have enough room left for another 250 calories of food. Would you have eaten a large, unseasoned baked potato (250 calories) if someone had put one in front of you at that point? Foods that stimulate the hedonic system have a well-known ability to increase food intake, and this effect can be replicated using drugs that activate these circuits directly (20). The reward system is what motivates you to get food and put it to your lips, every time you eat. When scientists shut it down in mice, they stop seeking food, even though they'll still eat if it's put into their mouths (21). The hedonic system influences how much you eat once you begin a meal (22). Together, reward and hedonic circuitry in the brain determine in large part how often you seek food, what foods you select, and how much you eat at a sitting.

Reward and hedonic systems, if stimulated in the right way by food or drugs, can increase food intake and body fatness. The marijuana 'munchies' (whose existence have been confirmed by science) are a good example of what happens when they're chemically stimulated via the CB1 cannabinoid receptor in the brain (23). One of the most effective weight loss drugs ever developed, Rimonabant, is basically 'reverse marijuana', blocking the very same CB1 receptor that marijuana activates. Although it clearly reduces food intake and body fatness, it has failed to gain FDA approval because of negative psychological side effects (big surprise).

The ability of reward and palatability to influence food intake and body weight is mediated by connections between reward/hedonic and energy homeostasis systems. For example, if you haven't eaten in a while, your brain detects declining energy stores and acts to increase food intake. It does this by increasing your motivation to obtain food, and your enjoyment of food once you obtain it—known as 'hunger', this sensation is caused in large part by energy homeostasis systems activating reward and hedonic systems. But the connection goes both ways. Reward and hedonic systems also influence energy homeostasis systems, such that excessively rewarding/palatable food can increase food intake and the level of body fat that's 'defended' by the brain (24, 25, 26, 27). According to findings from my own research group (lab of Michael W. Schwartz) and others, the hypothalamus can also develop inflammation and chronic cellular damage that likely contributes to the defense of a higher fat mass as well, contributing to fat gain and making fat loss more difficult (28, 29), but the reason for this is not yet clear.

Addiction is what happens when the reward system is overstimulated by drugs, sex, food or other high-reward stimuli. In susceptible people (about 3 percent of the US population), highly palatable/rewarding foods are quite literally addictive, leading to binge eating behavior. For the rest of us, these foods may not literally be addictive, but they do often drive us to eat them more than we think we should, despite negative consequences to our weight and health.

Living in a Toxic Food Environment

How has the American diet changed over the years, as obesity rates have soared? Taking a broad perspective, the largest change is that our food has become more like the 'cafeteria diet', awash in a large variety of packaged foods, restaurant meals and sweetened beverages. This is illustrated by the graph, showing the remarkable shift away from home-cooked food over the last 130 years. It shows the percentage of total food spending dedicated to food eaten at home, away from home, or as fast food between 1889 and 2009.

Diet trials have shown that a 'simple' diet, low in palatability and reward value, reduces hunger and causes fat loss in obese humans and animals, apparently by lowering the 'defended' level of fat mass (30, 31, 32, 33). This may be a reason why virtually any diet in which food choices are restricted (e.g., Paleo, vegan, fruitarian), including diametrically opposed approaches like low-fat and low-carbohydrate diets, can reduce food intake and body fatness in clinical trials. As stated by Nora Volkow, director of the National Institute on Drug Abuse, "The common denominator of such diets is that neither allows consumption of the very caloric and seductive foods that combine high fat with high carbohydrates" (34). Hyper-rewarding/palatable foods—candy, chocolate, ice cream, chips, cookies, cakes, fast food, sweetened beverages and pizzas—are uniquely fattening and should be the first foods to go in any fat loss attempt. Some people will benefit from further simplifying the diet.

Dietary changes over the last several decades have contributed to the obesity epidemic. The solution to this problem is at once simple and challenging. Returning to a diet of simple home-cooked food, made from minimally refined ingredients, would probably stop the obesity epidemic in its tracks, although it would not be enough to return all currently obese people to a lean state. The challenge is finding the time and discipline to do this while commercial junk foods and sweetened beverages are tasty, cheap and constantly under our noses.

Notes

1. http://www.cdc.gov/nchs/data/hestat/obesity_adult_07_08/obesity_adult_07_08.htm

2. http://www.ncbi.nlm.nih.gov/pubmed/19828708

3. http://www.ncbi.nlm.nih.gov/pubmed/19369382

4. http://www.ncbi.nlm.nih.gov/pubmed/11994393

5. http://www.ncbi.nlm.nih.gov/pubmed/1414963

6. http://ajpregu.physiology.org/content/259/3/R461

7. http://www.ncbi.nlm.nih.gov/pubmed/22238401

8. http://www.ncbi.nlm.nih.gov/pubmed/16988703

9. http://www.ncbi.nlm.nih.gov/pubmed/1013192

10. http://www.ncbi.nlm.nih.gov/pmc/articles/PMC3130193/

11. http://www.ncbi.nlm.nih.gov/pubmed/6634990

12. http://www.ncbi.nlm.nih.gov/pubmed/20186718

13. http://www.cnpp.usda.gov/DietaryGuidelines

14. http://www.ncbi.nlm.nih.gov/pubmed/1734670

15. http://www.ncbi.nlm.nih.gov/pubmed/7647825

16. http://www.ncbi.nlm.nih.gov/pubmed/7572735

17. http://www.ncbi.nlm.nih.gov/pubmed/2359760

18. http://www.ncbi.nlm.nih.gov/pubmed/8327611

19. http://www.ncbi.nlm.nih.gov/pubmed/22238401

20. http://www.ncbi.nlm.nih.gov/pubmed/17316713

21. http://www.ncbi.nlm.nih.gov/pubmed/8548806

22. http://www.ncbi.nlm.nih.gov/pubmed/14513063

23. http://www.ncbi.nlm.nih.gov/pubmed/3228283

24. http://www.ncbi.nlm.nih.gov/pubmed/12736179

25. http://www.ncbi.nlm.nih.gov/pubmed/1013218

26. http://www.ncbi.nlm.nih.gov/pubmed/22238401

27. http://www.ncbi.nlm.nih.gov/pubmed/11742822

28. http://www.ncbi.nlm.nih.gov/pubmed/22201683

29. http://www.ncbi.nlm.nih.gov/pubmed/18854155

30. http://www.ncbi.nlm.nih.gov/pubmed/1013218

31. http://www.ncbi.nlm.nih.gov/pubmed/5216999

32. http://www.ncbi.nlm.nih.gov/pubmed/4928686

33. http://www.ncbi.nlm.nih.gov/pubmed/11742822

34. http://www.ncbi.nlm.nih.gov/pubmed/15856062

| "A stressed person will put on more fat than a non-stressed person even when both eat the same number of calories."

The Rise in Obesity Is Due to Stress

Denise Cummins

In the following viewpoint, Denise Cummins explains that weight gain due to stress is not just a matter of people overeating when they are stressed, as is commonly believed. Stress alters the body's metabolism, she says, because it increases production of the hormone cortisol, which along with other undesirable effects causes fat cells to be shifted to the abdomen. Cortisol is also a direct cause of the diseases associated with obesity. In Cummins's opinion, dieting does not work because it does not take into account the effect of stress-produced cortisol; therefore, reducing obesity will require reducing Americans' stress level. Cummins is a research psychologist who has written several books and many scholarly publications.

As you read, consider the following questions:

1. In Cummins's opinion, what two comparisons between Americans and Europeans indicate that stress, rather than overeating, is primarily responsible for America's rise in obesity?

2. What evidence of the relationship between cortisol and abdominal fat, in addition to the production of cortisol by obese people, does Cummins mention?

3. What, as stated by Cummins, have experiments with rats shown about why stress makes people overeat?

Carbs. Fast Food. Supersized meals. Junk food. Eating too much, exercising too little. Genes. You've heard all about the role these factors play in the rise of obesity. So you've cut down on carbs, ramped up your exercise program, tailored your meals to suit your genes, and cooked meals at home. Yet you just get fatter. And sicker.

Here is the main reason why, in my opinion and that of many obesity researchers, Americans are so much fatter and so much sicker than the rest of the industrialized world. *Stress.*

No, I'm not just talking about deadlines and annoying in-laws. I'm talking about something more fundamental—pervasive, unrelenting, soul-crushing, daily stress. According to an on-going study[1] on stress in America conducted by the American Psychological Association, stress has become the new normal for life in the USA. Americans are more stressed and more unhappy than our counterparts in other countries. According to Columbia University's "First World Happiness Report,"[2] the United States does not even make the top 10 in happiness rankings, logging in at number 11, behind Denmark, Finland, Norway, the Netherlands, Canada, Switzerland, Sweden, New Zealand, Australia, and Ireland. And our level of happiness has remained about the same for decades. As Paul Rosch, a clinical professor of medicine and psychiatry at New

York Medical College and president of the nonprofit American Institute of Stress in Yonkers, N.Y., succinctly puts it, *"We have more or less accepted it as way of life . . ."*

To put this in more concrete terms, take a look at this graph[3] [not shown] from Food Service Warehouse.

What is apparent from the graph is that, although Americans eat more calories than anyone in the world, we do not eat substantially more than our 1st world counterparts in Europe. We consume only about 100 calories more per day than the French or Italians. Yet we are much, much fatter and sicker. Over a third of Americans (38%) are obese, but only about 20% of the French and 16% of Italians are, as you can see on this interactive graph[4] [not shown] from the International Association for the Study of Obesity.

When people hear that stress causes weight gain, they usually interpret it this way: People get stressed, so they eat more food (particularly sugary, fatty "comfort" food) to cope with their stress, and the extra calories cause them to gain weight. While there is some truth to this, what most people don't realize is that stress alone can cause us to put on fat by altering many metabolic functions. In other words, a stressed person will put on more fat than a non-stressed person even when both eat the same number of calories.

How Chronic Stress Makes Us Fat and Sick

According to exercise scientists Len Kravitz and colleagues at the University of New Mexico,[5] when stress is chronic, a cascade of hormonal pathways are activated that release large amounts of cortisol—a stress hormone—from the adrenals. Cortisol directly effects fat storage and weight gain in stressed individuals. It enhances lipogenesis (fat creation), break down of tissues, and suppression of the immune system. All of the things that make us fat and sick.

But high levels of cortisol also change our body shape dramatically by shifting fat to the abdomen from cells from the blood stream and other parts of the body. The fat that is created by high levels of cortisol is also more toxic than plain old subcutaneous fat (the normal fat under your skin). All fat cells contain an enzyme that converts inactive cortisone to active cortisol. But the gene that activates this conversion process is expressed more in obesity, particularly in deep abdominal fat cells. In fact, monkeys fed an American diet get fat—but those under chronic stress put on much more belly fat than less stressed monkeys. So it is almost as though toxic fat colonizes your abdomen, creating more of itself through the cortisol pathway that looks like this:

Stress - Cortisol - Enzyme activation - More, larger fat cells + more cortisol receptors.

This shift of fat toward the abdomen happens not just to overweight people but to normal-weight people as well. A study published in 2000[6] found that slender women who have high cortisol also were found to have more abdominal fat than their less stressed counterparts, indicating a definite causal link between cortisol and increased storage of abdominal fat. People who have diseases associated with extreme exposure to cortisol, such as Cushing's disease,[7] also have excessive amounts of visceral fat. This is why Dr. Oz commented in *First for Women*, "I can usually tell if someone is stressed out or not just by looking at their belly size."

The Negative Health Effects of Chronic Stress Don't Stop with Weight Gain

High levels of cortisol also cause high blood pressure, high cholesterol, and elevated glucose levels, laying the foundation for the development of cardiovascular disease, stroke, and diabetes—all of which have risen dramatically among Americans over the past few decades. According to the Centers for Disease Control and Prevention,[8] nearly 800,000 people die in the U.S. each year from cardiovascular disease, accounting for 1 in

3 deaths and more than $300 billion in direct medical costs and lost productivity. And statins are the leading prescription drugs sold in the U.S.

So how does chronic stress bring about this constellation of risk factors for heart disease?

It may surprise you to learn that only 25% of the cholesterol[9] in your body comes from what you eat. The other 75% is created in your very own liver[10] via an enzyme called HMG-CoA reductase. (Statins inhibit this enzyme, thereby inhibiting production of cholesterol. They also inhibit production of vitally important co-enzyme Q10.)

Now here is the interesting part: Insulin increases the production of LDL cholesterol.[11]

In fact, insulin and leptin resistance shift LDL particles from large harmless fluffy ones to small, dense, and dangerous ones.

Now the final piece of the puzzle: What increases insulin levels? Three primary factors: Carbohydrate consumption (which you already knew), sleep debt,[12] and chronic stress.[13] So chronic stress bumps your insulin levels, interferes with hormones that normally signal that you're full after you eat, and raises your bad cholesterol levels.

Why Dieting Dooms Us to Failure

If you are suffering from obesity, high cholesterol, metabolic syndrome, and high blood pressure, your doctor (and virtually everyone else around you) will begin sternly lecturing you about losing weight. Simple, right? Eat less, exercise more!

Well, unfortunately, this simplistic exhortation overlooks the true cause of your health woes, and instead places the blame squarely on your already overburdened shoulders. As you struggle unsuccessfully to reduce your weight, you will be lectured about your apparent gluttony, laziness, and lack of willpower. Your protestations that you are already trying desperately to lose weight will be met with smirks and frank incredulity. But here is why your efforts are failing.

Stress Hormone Levels Are High in Obese Children

Obese children naturally produce higher levels of a key stress hormone than their normal weight peers, according to new research.

The body produces the hormone cortisol when a person experiences stress. When a person faces frequent stress, cortisol and other stress hormones build up in the blood and, over time, can cause serious health problems. This study measured cortisol in scalp hair, which reflects long-term exposure and has been proposed to be a biomarker for stress. The study is the first to show obese children have chronically elevated levels of cortisol.

"We were surprised to find obese children, as young as age 8, already had elevated cortisol levels," said one of the study's authors, Erica van den Akker, of Erasmus MC-Sophia Children's Hospital in Rotterdam, the Netherlands. "By analyzing children's scalp hair, we were able to confirm high cortisol levels persisted over time.". . .

Obese subjects had an average cortisol concentration of 25 pg/mg in their scalp hair, compared to an average concentration of 17 pg/mg in the normal weight group. The hormone concentrations found in hair reflect cortisol exposure over the course of about one month. . . .

Van den Akker said, "We do not know whether obese children actually experience more psychological stress or if their bodies handle stress hormones differently. Answering these key questions will improve our understanding of childhood obesity and may change the way we treat it."

"Obese Children Have Higher Stress Hormone Levels than Normal Weight Peers,"
Endocrine Society, December 18, 2013.

Cortisol, sad to say, also increases appetite,[14] as well as cravings for sugary and fatty foods.

It interferes with satiety-regulating hormones[15] such as leptin and PYY so that when you eat these foods, it is difficult to stop because you don't feel sated.

Stress also leads to the release of neuropeptide Y[16] which stimulates abdominal fat formation and metabolic syndrome.

And that is why draconian diets and diets that restrict single macronutrients (low-fat or low-carbohydrate diets) usually backfire. They do not address high-circulating cortisol levels, so they do not normalize satiety feedback from the gastrointestinal tract to the brain. Because you don't feel sated but instead feel even more stressed from all the dieting, it is usually impossible for people to stick to these regimens.

This yo-yo dieting and weight loss failure is not particular to weak-willed humans. When stressed and unstressed rats were given free access to normal rat chow and sugar water,[17] the stressed ones will eat less healthy food, preferring instead to glug down the sugar water. (How do you stress a rat? Keep it in a confined space for several hours a day.) Not surprisingly, the stressed rats began accumulating belly fat. But then an interesting thing happened: Their cortisol levels began dropping. Dr. Mary Dallman, the lead author of this fascinating series of studies, explained the results this way: Gaining belly fat may be the body's coping mechanism for turning off the stress response. So your "stress eating" is not simply a dysfunctional coping mechanism learned from your parents, nor is it a psychological craving for love that is wrongfully addressed with food, nor any other explanations you may have heard. It is plainly and simply a short-term biologically based coping mechanism that is disastrous in the long run.

In the long run, chronic stress will overwhelm this short-term coping mechanism, as a series of studies[18] conducted by Dr. Carol Shively, PhD, of Wake Forest University on monkeys clearly shows. She fed female monkeys a high-fat "American style" diet, and compared various health indices of monkeys on top of the social hierarchy with those on the bottom rung. The results were sobering.

Monkeys on the bottom rung were more likely to put on belly fat than the high-ranking monkeys, despite eating the same fat-laden diet. They also showed more abdominal fat, more fat wrapped around organs, and more instances of metabolic syndrome. They were as likely as male monkeys to get heart disease, with large amounts of plaque clogging their arteries. All of this came from high levels of cortisol creating toxic abdominal fat. And all that cortisol came from living the stressed life that is "normal" on the bottom of a rigid social hierarchy.

What Is the Answer?

As this [viewpoint] plainly shows, we are not going to get thinner or healthier by simply cutting carbs, cutting calories, or increasing our exercise level. The body has numerous mechanisms, perfected over evolutionary time, to subvert these well-reasoned efforts to lose weight.

But we might just have a fighting chance if we reduce our stress levels. Accomplishing that requires understanding why—despite living in one of the richest countries in the world—we are so stressed.

Notes

1. http://www.apa.org/news/press/releases/stress/

2. http://www.earth.columbia.edu/articles/view/2960

3. http://www.foodservicewarehouse.com/calorie-viz/

4. http://www.worldobesity.org/

5. http://www.unm.edu/~lkravitz/Articlefolder/stresscortisol.html

6. http://journals.lww.com/psychosomaticmedicine/Abstract/2000/09000/Stress _and_Body_Shape__Stress_Induced_Cortisol.5.aspx

7. http://www.mayoclinic.org/diseases-conditions/cushing-syndrome/basics/ definition/con-20032115

8. http://blogs.cdc.gov/cdcworksforyou24-7/2013/01/cdc-looks-ahead-13-public
-health-issues-in-2013/

9. http://www.heart.org/HEARTORG/Conditions/Cholesterol/AboutCholesterol
/About-Cholesterol_UCM_001220_Article.jsp

10. http://themedicalbiochemistrypage.org/cholesterol.php

11. http://www.ncbi.nlm.nih.gov/pubmed/7945563

12. http://jap.physiology.org/content/99/5/2008.full

13. http://www.ncbi.nlm.nih.gov/pubmed/8287639

14. http://www.ncbi.nlm.nih.gov/pubmed/11070333

15. http://www.ncbi.nlm.nih.gov/pubmed/21098684

16. http://www.ncbi.nlm.nih.gov/pubmed/17603492

17. http://chc.ucsf.edu/pdf/2005_article_Dallman_BBI.pdf

18. http://www.ncbi.nlm.nih.gov/pubmed/19452515

> *"Antibiotics seem to increase [microbes']*
> *ability to break down carbs—and ulti-*
> *mately convert them to body fat."*

Antibiotics May Be Causing the Rise in Obesity

Tom Philpott

In the following viewpoint, Tom Philpott suggests that the antibiotics given to animals since the 1980s to fatten them for market may be having a similar effect on humans when retained in meat. Antibiotics affect the microbes that live in the digestive tracts of animals, and the residue from these antibiotics exists in the meat people eat. Also, he says, researchers have found that children who are given antibiotics in infancy have an increased chance of being overweight in early childhood. Philpott is a food columnist and the cofounder of Maverick Farms, a center for sustainable food education in North Carolina.

As you read, consider the following questions:

1. In the experiment described by Philpott, what effect did regular low doses of antibiotics have on mice?

2. In the study described by Philpott, what was learned about the long-term effect of antibiotics given to babies?

3. Why does Philpott question the safety of the amount of
   antibiotic residue the FDA allows in meat?

Like hospital patients, US farm animals tend to be confined
to tight spaces and dosed with antibiotics. But that's where
the similarities end. Hospitals dole out antibiotics to save
lives. On America's factory-scale meat farms, the goal is to fatten animals for their date at the slaughterhouse.

And it turns out that antibiotics help with the fattening
process. Back in the 1940s, scientists discovered that regular
low doses of antibiotics increased "feed efficiency"—that is,
they caused animals to put on more weight per pound of
feed. No one understood why, but farmers seized on this un-
expected benefit. By the 1980s, feed laced with small amounts
of the drugs became de rigueur [required] as US meat production shifted increasingly to factory farms. In 2009, an estimated 80 percent of the antibiotics sold in the United States
went to livestock.

This year [2013], scientists may have finally figured out
why small doses of antibiotics "promote growth," as the industry puts it: They make subtle changes to what's known as the
"gut microbiome," the teeming universe populated by billions
of microbes that live within the digestive tracts of animals. In
recent research, the microbiome has been emerging as key
regulator of health from immune-related disorders like aller-
gies and asthma to the ability to fight off pathogens.

In an August study published in *Nature*, a team of New
York University [NYU] researchers subjected mice to regular
low doses of antibiotics—just like cows, pigs, and chickens get
on factory farms. The result: After seven weeks, the drugged
mice had a different composition of microbiota in their guts
than the control group—and they had gained 10 to 15 percent
more fat mass.

Why? "Microbes in our gut are able to digest certain carbohydrates that we're not able to," says NYU researcher and

The FDA Is Phasing Out Use of Antibiotics to Fatten Animals

[As of December 2013] the Food and Drug Administration (FDA) is implementing a voluntary plan with industry to phase out the use of certain antibiotics for enhanced food production.

Antibiotics are added to the animal feed or drinking water of cattle, hogs, poultry and other food-producing animals to help them gain weight faster or use less food to gain weight....

It is not entirely understood how these drugs make animals grow faster. The drugs are primarily added to feed, although they are sometimes added to the animals' drinking water.

Bacteria evolve to survive threats to their existence. In both humans and animals, even appropriate therapeutic uses of antibiotics can promote the development of drug-resistant bacteria. When such bacteria enter the food supply, they can be transferred to the people who eat food from the treated animal.

"Phasing Out Certain Antibiotic Use in Farm Animals,"
Food and Drug Administration, December 11, 2013.

study coauthor Ilseung Cho. Antibiotics seem to increase those bugs' ability to break down carbs—and ultimately convert them to body fat. As a result, the antibiotic-fed mice "actually extracted more energy from the same diet" as the control mice, he says. That's great if you're trying to fatten a giant barn full of hogs. But what about that two-legged species that's often exposed to antibiotics?

Interestingly, the NYU team has produced another recent paper looking at just that question. They analyzed data from a

UK [United Kingdom] study in the early '90s to see if they could find a correlation between antibiotic exposure and kids' weight. The study involved more than 11,000 kids, about a third of whom had been prescribed antibiotics to treat an infection before the age of six months. The results: The babies who had been exposed to antibiotics had a 22 percent higher chance of being overweight at age three than those who hadn't (though by age seven the effect had worn off).

The connection raises another obvious question: Are we being exposed to tiny levels of antibiotics through residues in the meat we eat—and are they altering our gut flora? It turns out that the Food and Drug Administration [FDA] maintains tolerance limits for antibiotic residue levels, above which meat isn't supposed to be released to the public. But Keeve Nachman, who researches antibiotic use in the meat industry for the Johns Hopkins Center for a Livable Future, told me that the FDA sets these limits based solely on research financed and conducted by industry—and it refuses to release the complete data to the public or consider independent research.

"We may not understand the biological relevance of exposures through consuming meat at those levels," he says. Indeed, a recent European study showed that tiny levels of antibiotics could have an effect on microorganisms. The researchers took some meat, subjected it to antibiotic residues near the US limit, and used a traditional technique to turn it into sausage, inoculating it with lactic-acid-producing bacteria. In normal sausage making, the lactic acid from the starter bacteria spreads through the meat and kills pathogens like *E. coli*. The researchers found, though, that the antibiotic traces were strong enough to impede the starter bacteria, while still letting the *E. coli* flourish. In other words, even at very low levels, antibiotics can blast "good" bacteria—and promote deadly germs.

Nachman stressed that we simply don't have sufficient information to tell whether the meat we eat is messing with our gut microbiome. But, he adds, "It's not an unreasonable suspicion." If that's not enough to churn your stomach, there's also the fact that drug-resistant bugs—which often emerge in antibiotic-dosed livestock on factory farms—are increasingly common: Remember the super-salmonella that caused Cargill to recall 36 million pounds of ground turkey last year? Luckily for me, it's unlikely that drug-laced meat will mess with my gut. I think I've lost my appetite.

> *"The role of environmental chemicals in obesity has garnered increased attention in academic and policy spheres, and was recently acknowledged by the [White House] Task Force on Childhood Obesity."*

Environmental Chemicals May Be Causing the Rise in Obesity

Wendee Holtcamp

In the following viewpoint, Wendee Holtcamp discusses new discoveries about how chemicals in the environment may be contributing to obesity. Many such chemicals, which are called obesogens, have been found to alter metabolic processes in laboratory animals, causing them—and often their offspring—to gain weight. Research into this phenomenon is just beginning, and there is not enough data yet to determine the extent to which obesogens affect humans, but in time enough may be learned for obesity to be curbed by reducing exposure to these chemicals. Holtcamp is a Houston-based science writer who has written for many national publications.

Wendee Holtcamp, "Obesogens: An Environmental Link to Obesity," *Environmental Health Perspectives*, 2012.

As you read, consider the following questions:

1. According to Holtcamp, how and when did the term "obesogen" originate?

2. About how many different chemicals have been shown to be risk factors for weight gain if an animal is exposed to them during its development?

3. In the opinion of biology professor Bruce Blumberg, will people exposed to obesogens prior to birth or in infancy be fat for the rest of their lives?

Obesity has risen steadily in the United States over the past 150 years, with a marked uptick in recent decades. In the United States today more than 35% of adults and nearly 17% of children aged 2–19 years are obese. Obesity plagues people not just in the United States but worldwide, including, increasingly, developing countries. Even animals—pets, laboratory animals, and urban rats—have experienced increases in average body weight over the past several decades, trends not necessarily explained by diet and exercise. In the words of Robert H. Lustig, a professor of clinical pediatrics at the University of California, San Francisco, "[E]ven those at the lower end of the BMI [body mass index] curve are gaining weight. Whatever is happening is happening to everyone, suggesting an environmental trigger."

Many in the medical and exercise physiology communities remain wedded to poor diet and lack of exercise as the sole causes of obesity. However, researchers are gathering convincing evidence of chemical "obesogens"—dietary, pharmaceutical, and industrial compounds that may alter metabolic processes and predispose some people to gain weight. . . .

The role of environmental chemicals in obesity has garnered increased attention in academic and policy spheres, and was recently acknowledged by the [White House] Task Force on Childhood Obesity and the National Institutes of Health

(NIH) strategic plan for obesity research. "Over the past ten years, and especially the past five years, there's been a flurry of new data," says Kristina Thayer, director of the Office of Health Assessment and Translation at the National Toxicology Program (NTP). "There are many studies in both humans and animals. The NTP found real biological plausibility." In 2011 the NIH launched a 3-year effort to fund research exploring the role of environmental chemical exposures in obesity, type 2 diabetes mellitus, and metabolic syndrome.

Multiple Modes of Action

The main role of fat cells is to store energy and release it when needed. Scientists also now know that fat tissue acts as an endocrine organ, releasing hormones related to appetite and metabolism. Research to date suggests different obesogenic compounds may have different mechanisms of action, some affecting the number of fat cells, others the size of fat cells, and still others the hormones that affect appetite, satiety, food preferences, and energy metabolism. Some obesogenic effects may pass on to later generations through epigenetic changes, heritable modifications to DNA and histone proteins that affect when and how genes are expressed in cells, without altering the actual genetic code.

Bruce Blumberg, a biology professor at the University of California, Irvine, coined the term "obesogen" in 2006 when he discovered that tin-based compounds known as organotins predisposed laboratory mice to gain weight. "If you give tributyltin [TBT] to pregnant mice, their offspring are heavier than those not exposed," he says. "We've altered the physiology of these offspring, so even if they eat normal food, they get slightly fatter."

Human exposure and health-effect data are relatively rare for organotins, but studies have documented the presence of these compounds in human blood, milk, and liver samples. Although phased out as a biocide and marine antifouling agent, TBT is still used as a wood preservative and, along with dibutyltin, as a stabilizer in polyvinyl chloride [PVC]; it pollutes many waterways and contaminates seafood.

Blumberg was studying endocrine disruptors in the early 2000s when he heard at a meeting in Japan that TBT causes sex reversal in multiple fish species. "I decided to test whether TBT activated known nuclear receptors, expecting it to activate a sex steroid receptor," Blumberg says. Instead, it activated peroxisome proliferator-activated receptor gamma (PPARγ), the master regulator of adipogenesis, the process of creating adipocytes, or fat cells. . . .

"If you activate PPARγ in a preadipocyte, it becomes a fat cell. If it already is a fat cell, it puts more fat in the cell," Blumberg says. "TBT is changing the metabolism of exposed animals, predisposing them to make more and bigger fat cells." . . . "The insidious thing is that our animals are exposed *in utero* to TBT, then never again, yet TBT caused a permanent effect."

A Growing List of Potential Obesogens

Obesity is strongly linked with exposure to risk factors during fetal and infant development. "There are between fifteen and twenty chemicals that have been shown to cause weight gain, mostly from developmental exposure," says Jerry Heindel, who leads the extramural research program in obesity at the National Institute of Environmental Health Sciences (NIEHS). However, some obesogens have been hypothesized to affect adults, with epidemiologic studies linking levels of chemicals in human blood with obesity and studies showing that certain pharmaceuticals activate PPARγ receptors.

Chemical pesticides in food and water, particularly atrazine and DDE (dichlorodiphenyldichloroethylene—a DDT breakdown product), have been linked to increased BMI [body mass index] in children and insulin resistance in rodents. Certain pharmaceuticals, such as the diabetes drug Avandia®

(rosiglitazone), have been linked to weight gain in humans and animals, as have a handful of dietary obesogens, including the soy phytoestrogen genistein and monosodium glutamate.

Most known or suspected obesogens are endocrine disruptors. Many are widespread, and exposures are suspected or confirmed to be quite common. In one 2010 study, Kurunthachalam Kannan, a professor of environmental sciences at the University at Albany, State University of New York, documented organotins in a designer handbag, wallpaper, vinyl blinds, tile, and vacuum cleaner dust collected from 24 houses. Phthalates, plasticizers that also have been related to obesity in humans, occur in many PVC items as well as in scented items such as air fresheners, laundry products, and personal care products.

One of the earliest links between human fetal development and obesity arose from studies of exposure to cigarette smoke *in utero*. Although secondhand-smoke exposure has decreased by more than half over the past 20 years, an estimated 40% of nonsmoking Americans still have nicotine by-products in their blood, suggesting exposure remains widespread. Babies born to smoking mothers are frequently underweight, but these same infants tend to make up for it by putting on more weight during infancy and childhood. "If a baby is born relatively small for its gestational age, it tries to 'play catch-up' as it develops and grows," explains Retha Newbold, a developmental biologist now retired from the NTP.

This pattern of catch-up growth is often observed with developmental exposure to chemicals now thought to be obesogens, including diethylstilbestrol (DES), which Newbold spent the last 30 years studying, using mice as an experimental model. Doctors prescribed DES, a synthetic estrogen, to millions of pregnant women from the late 1930s through the 1970s to prevent miscarriage. The drug caused adverse effects in these women's children, who often experienced reproductive tract abnormalities; "DES daughters" also had a higher risk of reproductive problems, vaginal cancer in adolescence, and breast cancer in adulthood. Newbold discovered that low doses of DES administered to mice pre- or neonatally also were associated with weight gain, altered expression of obesity-related genes, and modified hormone levels.

"What we're seeing is there's not a difference in the number of fat cells, but the cell itself is larger after exposure to DES," Newbold says. "There was also a difference in how [fat cells] were distributed—where they went, how they lined up, and their orientation with each other. The mechanism for fat distribution and making fat cells are set up during fetal and neonatal life."

High-Profile Exposures

Animal studies have also implicated another suspected obesogen: bisphenol A (BPA), which is found in medical devices, in the lining of some canned foods, and in cash register receipts. "BPA reduces the number of fat cells but programs them to incorporate more fat, so there are fewer but very large fat cells," explains University of Missouri biology professor Frederick vom Saal, who has studied BPA for the past 15 years. "In animals, BPA exposure is producing in animals the kind of outcomes that we see in humans born light at birth: an increase in abdominal fat and glucose intolerance.". . .

Still another widespread obesogen is perfluorooctanoic acid (PFOA), a potential endocrine disruptor and known PPARγ agonist. "Pretty much everyone in the U.S. has it in their blood, kids having higher levels than adults, probably because of their habits. They crawl on carpets, on furniture, and put things in their mouth more often," explains NIEHS biologist Suzanne Fenton. PFOA is a surfactant used for reduction of friction, and it is also used in nonstick cookware, Gore-Tex™ waterproof clothing, Scotchgard™ stain repellent on carpeting, mattresses, and microwavable food items. . . .

Fenton studied how PFOA levels similar to those in the tainted drinking water affected the hormone levels and weight of rodent offspring exposed *in utero*. "We gave pregnant mice PFOA only during pregnancy. It has a long half-life, so it hangs around during lactation and gets delivered in milk to babies," Fenton says. "Once the offspring reached adulthood, they became obese, reaching significantly higher weight levels than controls." . . .

Eye on Prevention

If exposure during pregnancy predisposes people to gain weight, can diet and exercise ultimately make any difference? Blumberg does not consider the situation hopeless. "I would not want to say that obesogen exposure takes away free will or dooms you to be fat," he says. "However, it will change your metabolic set points for gaining weight. If you have more fat cells and propensity to make more fat cells, and if you eat the typical high-carbohydrate, high-fat diet we eat [in the United States], you probably will get fat."

Blumberg postulates that the effects of early-life exposure are irreversible, and those people will fight a lifelong battle of the bulge. However, if such people reduce their exposure to obesogens, they will also reduce health effects that may arise from ongoing adulthood exposures. Blumberg believes it's good to reduce exposure to all kinds of endocrine-disrupting chemicals. "Eat organic, filter water, minimize plastic in your life," he says. "If there's no benefit and some degree of risk, why expose yourself and your family?"

Heindel hopes the NIH's new grant-making effort will yield important discoveries. "It's a very new field, and people are always skeptical of new fields," he says. "It's up to us to get more data to show that chemicals are actually interfering with the endocrine system that controls weight gain and metabolism. And there's still the question of how important is this to humans. We're never going to know until we get more data."

"What if this was really true and chemicals are having a significant effect on obesity?" muses Heindel. "If we could show environmental chemicals play a major role, then we could work on reducing exposure during sensitive windows, and that could have a huge effect [on obesity prevalence]." It would change the focus from treating adults who are already obese to preventing obesity before it starts—a fundamental shift in thinking about obesity.

| "*Many researchers believe that personal gluttony and laziness cannot be the entire explanation for humanity's global weight gain.*"

Many Complex Factors Contribute to the Rise in Obesity

David Berreby

In the following viewpoint, David Berreby explains that scientists are by no means as unanimous about the causes of the rise in human obesity as public health agencies maintain. Scientists now believe that there must be much more involved than the amount of food people eat and their level of physical activity. The theory that it is merely a matter of diet and exercise cannot explain the fact that wild animals, too, are heavier than in the past, nor can it explain the differences in weight gain among socioeconomic groups. Therefore, Berreby says, researchers are investigating many other factors that may be direct causes of the trend toward obesity. Berreby is a science writer who has contributed essays to many national publications, and he writes the blog Mind Matters.

As you read, consider the following questions:

1. Why, according to Berreby, do many researchers believe that public health authorities' focus on personal conduct in combating obesity is a waste of time and money?

2. What, in Berreby's opinion, makes the theory that not all calories are equal especially significant?

3. How, according to Berreby's explanation, could modern heating and air-conditioning be contributing to the rise in obesity?

We appear to have a public consensus that excess body weight (defined as a body mass index [BMI] of 25 or above) and obesity (BMI of 30 or above) are consequences of individual choice. It is undoubtedly true that societies are spending vast amounts of time and money on this idea. It is also true that the masters of the universe in business and government seem attracted to it, perhaps because stern self-discipline is how many of them attained their status. What we *don't* know is whether the theory is actually correct.

Of course, that's not the impression you will get from the admonishments of public health agencies and wellness businesses. They are quick to assure us that 'science says' obesity is caused by individual choices about food and exercise. As the mayor of New York, Michael Bloomberg, recently put it, defending his proposed ban on large cups for sugary drinks: 'If you want to lose weight, don't eat. This is not medicine, it's thermodynamics. If you take in more than you use, you store it.' (Got that? It's not complicated *medicine*, it's simple *physics*, the most sciencey science of all.)

Yet the scientists who study the biochemistry of fat and the epidemiologists who track weight trends are not nearly as unanimous as Bloomberg makes out. In fact, many researchers believe that personal gluttony and laziness *cannot* be the entire explanation for humanity's global weight gain. Which means, of course, that they think at least some of the official focus on personal conduct is a waste of time and money. As Richard L. Atkinson, emeritus professor of medicine and nutritional sciences at the University of Wisconsin and editor of the *International Journal of Obesity*, put it in 2005: 'The previous belief of many lay people and health professionals that obesity is simply the result of a lack of willpower and an inability to discipline eating habits is no longer defensible.'

Many Species Are Getting Fatter

Consider, for example, this troublesome fact, reported in 2010 by the biostatistician David B. Allison and his coauthors at the University of Alabama in Birmingham: Over the past 20 years or more, as the American people were getting fatter, so were America's marmosets. As were laboratory macaques, chimpanzees, vervet monkeys and mice, as well as domestic dogs, domestic cats, and domestic and feral rats from both rural and urban areas. In fact, the researchers examined records on those eight species and found that average weight for every one had increased. The marmosets gained an average of nine per cent per decade. Lab mice gained about 11 per cent per decade. Chimps, for some reason, are doing especially badly: their average body weight had risen 35 per cent per decade. Allison, who had been hearing about an unexplained rise in the average weight of lab animals, was nonetheless surprised by the consistency across so many species. 'Virtually in every population of animals we looked at, that met our criteria, there was the same upward trend,' he told me.

It isn't hard to imagine that people who are eating more themselves are giving more to their spoiled pets, or leaving sweeter, fattier garbage for street cats and rodents. But such results don't explain why the weight gain is also occurring in species that human beings don't pamper, such as animals in labs, whose diets are strictly controlled. In fact, lab animals' lives are so precisely watched and measured that the researchers can rule out accidental human influence: records show those creatures gained weight over decades without any significant change in their diet or activities. Obviously, if animals are getting heavier along with us, it can't just be that they're eating more Snickers bars and driving to work most days. On the contrary, the trend suggests some widely shared cause, beyond the control of individuals, which is contributing to obesity across many species.

Such a global hidden factor (or factors) might help to explain why most people gain weight gradually, over decades, in seeming contradiction of Bloomberg's thermodynamics. This slow increase in fat stores would suggest that they are eating only a tiny bit more each month than they use in fuel. But if that were so, as Jonathan C.K. Wells, professor of child nutrition at University College London, has pointed out, it would be easy to lose weight. . . .

Many other aspects of the worldwide weight gain are also difficult to square with the 'it's-just-thermodynamics' model. In rich nations, obesity is more prevalent in people with less money, education and status. Even in some poor countries, according to a survey published last year in the *International Journal of Obesity*, increases in weight over time have been concentrated among the least well-off. And the extra weight is unevenly distributed among the sexes, too. In a study published in the *Social Science and Medicine* journal last year, Wells and his coauthors found that, in a sample that spanned 68 nations, for every two obese men there were three obese women. Moreover, the researchers found that higher levels of female obesity correlated with higher levels of gender inequality in each nation. Why, if body weight is a matter of individual decisions about what to eat, should it be affected by differences in wealth or by relations between the sexes?

To make sense of all this, the purely thermodynamic model must appeal to complicated indirect effects. The story might go like this: being poor is stressful, and stress makes you eat, and the cheapest food available is the stuff with a lot of 'empty calories', therefore poorer people are fatter than the better-off. These wheels-within-wheels are required because the mantra of the thermodynamic model is that 'a calorie is a calorie is a calorie': who you are and what you eat are irrelevant to whether you will add fat to your frame. The badness of a 'bad' food such as a Cheeto is that it makes calorie intake easier than it would be with broccoli or an apple.

Not All Calories Are Equal

Yet a number of researchers have come to believe, as Wells himself wrote earlier this year in the *European Journal of Clinical Nutrition*, that 'all calories are not equal'. The problem with diets that are heavy in meat, fat or sugar is not solely that they pack a lot of calories into food; it is that they alter the biochemistry of fat storage and fat expenditure, tilting the body's system in favour of fat storage. Wells notes, for example, that sugar, trans fats and alcohol have all been linked to changes in 'insulin signalling', which affects how the body processes carbohydrates. This might sound like a merely technical distinction. In fact, it's a paradigm shift: if the problem isn't the number of calories but rather biochemical influences on the body's fat-making and fat-storage processes, then sheer quantity of food or drink are not the all-controlling determinants of weight gain. If candy's chemistry tilts you toward fat, then the fact that you eat it at all may be as important as the amount of it you consume.

More importantly, 'things that alter the body's fat metabolism' is a much wider category than food. Sleeplessness and stress, for instance have been linked to disturbances in the effects of leptin, the hormone that tells the brain that the body has had enough to eat. What other factors might be at work? Viruses, bacteria and industrial chemicals have all entered the sights of obesity research. So have such aspects of modern life as electric light, heat and air-conditioning. All of these have been proposed, with some evidence, as *direct* causes of weight gain: the line of reasoning is not that stress causes you to eat more, but rather that it causes you to gain weight by directly altering the activities of your cells. If some or all of these factors are indeed contributing to the worldwide fattening trend, then the thermodynamic model is wrong.

There May Be Many Causes

Lurking behind these prime suspects [stress, antibiotics, and industrial chemicals], there are the fugitive possibilities—what David B. Allison and another band of coauthors recently called the 'roads less travelled' of obesity research. For example, consider the increased control civilisation gives people over the temperature of their surroundings. There is a 'thermoneutral zone' in which a human body can maintain its normal internal temperature without expending energy. Outside this zone, when it's hot enough to make you sweat or cold enough to make you shiver, the body has to expend energy to maintain homeostasis. Temperatures above and below the neutral zone have been shown to cause both humans and animals to burn fat, and hotter conditions also have an indirect effect: they make people eat less. A restaurant on a warm day whose air-conditioning breaks down will see a sharp decline in sales (yes, someone did a study). Perhaps we are getting fatter in part because our heaters and air conditioners are keeping us in the thermoneutral zone.

And what about light? A study by Laura Fonken and colleagues at the Ohio State University in Columbus, published in 2010 in the *Proceedings of the National Academy of Sciences*, reported that mice exposed to extra light (experiencing either no dark at all or a sort of semidarkness instead of total night) put on nearly 50 per cent more weight than mice fed the same diet who lived on a normal night-day cycle of alternating light and dark. This effect might be due to the constant light robbing the rodents of their natural cues about when to eat. Wild mice eat at night, but night-deprived mice might have been eating during the day, at the 'wrong' time physiologically. It's possible that widespread electrification is promoting obesity by making humans eat at night, when our ancestors were asleep.

There is also the possibility that obesity could quite literally be contagious. A virus called Ad-36 [adenovirus 36], known for causing eye and respiratory infections in people, also has the curious property of causing weight gain in chickens, rats, mice and monkeys. Of course, it would be unethical to test for this effect on humans, but it is now known that antibodies to the virus are found in a much higher percentage of obese people than in people of normal weight. A research review by Tomohide Yamada and colleagues at the University of Tokyo in Japan, published last year in the journal *PLoS One*, found that people who had been infected with Ad-36 had significantly higher BMI than those who hadn't.

As with viruses, so with bacteria. Experiments by Lee Kaplan and colleagues at Massachusetts General Hospital in Boston earlier this year found that bacteria from mice that have lost weight will, when placed in other mice, apparently cause those mice to lose weight, too. And a study in humans by Ruchi Mathur and colleagues at the Cedars-Sinai Medical Center in Los Angeles, published in the *Journal of Clinical Endocrinology and Metabolism* earlier this year, found that those who were overweight were more likely than others to have elevated populations of a gut microorganisms called *Methanobrevibacter smithii*. The researchers speculated that these organisms might in fact be especially good at digesting food, yielding up more nutrients and thus contributing to weight gain.

No one has claimed, or should claim, that any of these 'roads less taken' is *the* one true cause of obesity, to drive out the false idol of individual choice. Neither should we imagine that the existence of alternative theories means that governments can stop trying to forestall a major public health menace. These theories are important for a different reason. Their very existence—the fact that they are plausible, with some supporting evidence and suggestions for further research—gives lie to the notion that obesity is a closed question, on which science has pronounced its final word. It might be that every one of the 'roads less travelled' contributes to global obesity; it might be that some do in some places and not in others. The openness of the issue makes it clear that obesity *isn't* a simple school physics experiment. . . .

Today's priests of obesity prevention proclaim with confidence and authority that they have the answer. So did Bruno Bettelheim in the 1950s, when he blamed autism on mothers with cold personalities. So, for that matter, did the clerics of 18th-century Lisbon, who blamed earthquakes on people's sinful ways. History is not kind to authorities whose mistaken dogmas cause unnecessary suffering and pointless effort, while ignoring the real causes of trouble. And the history of the obesity era has yet to be written.

Periodical and Internet Sources Bibliography

The following articles have been selected to supplement the diverse views presented in this chapter.

Paula J. Caplan — "Elephant in the Living Room: Obesity Epidemic and Psychiatric Drugs," *Science Isn't Golden—Psychology Today* (blog), May 13, 2011.

Robb Dunn — "Obesity Virus, Fat Chickens and Life's Mysteries," *Pacific Standard*, May 21, 2011.

Dan Hurley — "A New Suspect in the Obesity Epidemic: Our Brains," *Discover*, June 2011.

Brandon Keim — "Antibiotics Might Be Fueling Obesity Epidemic," *Wired*, August 22, 2012.

Pagan Kennedy — "The Fat Drug," *New York Times*, March 8, 2014.

Sendhil Mullainathan — "The Co-Villains Behind Obesity's Rise," *New York Times*, November 11, 2013.

Barbara Natterson-Horowitz and Kathryn Bowers — "Our Animal Natures," *New York Times*, June 10, 2012.

Lynn Peeples — "BPA's Obesity and Diabetes Link Strengthened by New Study," *Huffington Post*, February 15, 2012.

Gary Taubes — "Why the Campaign to Stop America's Obesity Crisis Keeps Failing," *Newsweek*, May 7, 2012.

Honor Whiteman — "Obesity May Be Caused by 'Hunger Gene,'" *Medical News Today*, October 27, 2013.

For Further Discussion

Chapter 1

1. Dan Carroll contends that the United States' obesity epidemic has a negative impact on the nation's economy. In your opinion, does the viewpoint provide sufficient evidence to support this argument? Explain your answer.

2. Linda Bacon argues that the weight loss industry and pharmaceutical companies promote the belief that obesity is harmful to raise their profits. Do you agree that the dangers of obesity are exaggerated by these industries for financial gain? Why, or why not?

Chapter 2

1. Mark J. Holland points out that the American Medical Association (AMA) has recently classified obesity as a disease. Why does Holland believe this new classification will benefit obese patients? Do you agree or disagree with Holland's argument? Explain.

2. Sara Stein reports on the AMA's decision to classify obesity as a disease. She strongly favors this decision. After reading Stein's viewpoint, are you in favor of the decision as well? Explain your answer.

3. S.E. Smith claims that being overweight is not always unhealthy. Smith argues that an overweight person who eats a healthy diet and maintains a consistent weight is healthy. Do you agree or disagree? Provide reasons to support your answer.

Chapter 3

1. Lawrence O. Gostin claims that the government has the power, and the responsibility, to regulate sugary drinks. However, Jonathan S. Tobin argues that the government

has no right to regulate personal choices. In your opinion, which author offers the more persuasive argument? Give examples from the viewpoints to support your answer.

2. Michael Smith contends that reducing obesity is more important than freedom of choice. In your view, should the public sacrifice freedom of choice in order to fight obesity? Why, or why not?

Chapter 4

1. As Kristina Fiore reports, a study found that overeating is the main cause of the obesity epidemic. Timothy S. Church and his coauthors assert that the decrease in occupations requiring physical activity accounts for a large portion of the increase in average weight. With which viewpoint do you agree, and why?

2. Stephan J. Guyenet maintains that Americans should eat a less palatable diet. What is Guyenet's reasoning behind this assertion? Do you agree with Guyenet's argument? Explain.

3. Tom Philpott suggests that humans may gain weight from eating meat that comes from livestock that were given antibiotics to fatten them. In your opinion, does this seem like a plausible argument to explain the rise in human obesity? Explain your answer.

Organizations to Contact

The editors have compiled the following list of organizations concerned with the issues debated in this book. The descriptions are derived from materials provided by the organizations. All have publications or information available for interested readers. The list was compiled on the date of publication of the present volume; the information provided here may change. Be aware that many organizations take several weeks or longer to respond to inquiries, so allow as much time as possible.

American Obesity Treatment Association (AOTA)
117 Anderson Court, Suite 1, Dothan, AL 36303
(334) 403-4057
e-mail: info@americanobesity.org
website: www.americanobesity.org

The American Obesity Treatment Association (AOTA) is a nonprofit organization that seeks to prevent and treat obesity. AOTA also works to educate and bring together people who are struggling with or affected by obesity. The organization places special emphasis on childhood obesity. AOTA offers a free monthly e-newsletter, *American Obesity*, along with brochures and a body mass index (BMI) calculator. Its website also has an online bookstore with numerous titles, including *The Evolution of Obesity* and *Management of Childhood Obesity*.

Association for Size Diversity and Health (ASDAH)
PO Box 3093, Redwood City, CA 94064
(877) 576-1102
website: www.sizediversityandhealth.org

The Association for Size Diversity and Health (ASDAH) is an international professional organization that promotes education, research, and services that enhance health and well-being. ASDAH and its members are committed to the Health at Every Size (HAES) principles, which include weight inclusivity, health enhancement, respectful care, eating for well-being, and life-enhancing movement. The ASDAH blog has close to 750 followers and allows contributors to share their experiences with the HAES approach. ASDAH also provides a wealth of publications on its website, including "Overweight and Obese Children Eat Less than Their Healthy Weight Peers," "Coming Out as Fat: Rethinking Stigma," and "Fighting Obesity or Obese Persons? Public Perceptions of Obesity-Related Health Messages."

Campaign to End Obesity

805 Fifteenth Street NW, Suite 650, Washington, DC   20005
(202) 466-8100
website: obesitycampaign.org

The Campaign to End Obesity is an organization that works to reverse the obesity epidemic by confronting the issue at the national policy level. The campaign provides information and guidance to policy makers to encourage them to make the necessary policy changes to reverse the epidemic. The campaign's website provides several resources, including "Obesity Facts & Resources." The website also offers a link that provides up-to-date news on obesity in America.

Center for Science in the Public Interest (CSPI)

1220 L Street NW, Suite 300, Washington, DC   20005
(202) 332-9110 • fax: (202) 265-4954
website: www.cspinet.org

The Center for Science in the Public Interest (CSPI) seeks to be the organized voice of the American public on nutrition, food safety, health, and other issues. CSPI educates the public, advocates government policies that are consistent with scientific evidence on health and environmental issues, and counters the industry's powerful influence on public opinion and public policies. CSPI supports food labeling campaigns and government efforts aimed at reducing the amount of sugar, salt, and fat Americans eat. On its website, CSPI offers many news articles, as well as a newsletter, *Nutrition Action Healthletter*, which is the largest circulation health and nutrition newsletter in North America.

Centers for Disease Control and Prevention (CDC) Division of Nutrition, Physical Activity, and Obesity (DNPAO)

1600 Clifton Road, Atlanta, GA 30333
(800) 232-4636
e-mail: cdcinfo@cdc.gov
website: www.cdc.gov/nccdphp/dnpao

The Centers for Disease Control and Prevention (CDC) is part of the National Institutes of Health (NIH), Department of Health and Human Services (DHHS). Its Division of Nutrition, Physical Activity, and Obesity (DNPAO) addresses the role of nutrition and physical activity in improving public health. DNPAO activities include health promotion, research, training, and education. The DNPAO website contains an array of publications and resources, as well as a link to Choose MyPlate.gov. DNPAO also maintains an overweight and obesity webpage, on which it provides research-based information for consumers.

Let's Move!

website: www.letsmove.gov

Let's Move! is a comprehensive initiative focused on solving the problem of childhood obesity within a generation. Launched by First Lady Michelle Obama, the initiative has five basic principles: creating a healthy start for children; empowering parents and caregivers; providing healthy food in schools; improving access to healthy, affordable foods; and increasing physical activity. The Let's Move! website offers many videos and other resources, including "First Lady Column on Physical Activity" and "Let's Move! Get Involved Factsheet."

Obesity Action Coalition (OAC)

4511 North Himes Avenue, Suite 250, Tampa, FL 33614
(800) 717-3117

e-mail: info@obesityaction.org
website: www.obesityaction.org

The Obesity Action Coalition (OAC) is a not-for-profit organization that educates not only obesity patients, but also their
family members and the public. It provides links to resources
and obesity support groups throughout the United States.
OAC works against the stigma of obesity and is an advocate
for safe and effective obesity treatment. Its website includes
many brochures and offers the official magazine of the OAC,
Your Weight Matters.

Obesity Society
8757 Georgia Avenue, Suite 1320, Silver Spring, MD   20910
(301) 563-6526 • fax: (301) 563-6595
website: www.obesity.org

The Obesity Society is the leading scientific organization dedicated to the study of obesity. Since 1982, the society has been
committed to encouraging research on the causes and treatment of obesity and to keeping the medical community and
public informed of new advances. The Obesity Society offers
Obesity, its official journal, as well as its monthly e-newsletter.
On its website, the society publishes position statements, such
as "The Need for Increased Obesity Research Funding" and
"Solutions: Eradicating America's Obesity Epidemic."

Robert Wood Johnson Foundation (RWJF)
Route 1 and College Road East, PO Box 2316
Princeton, NJ   08543-2316
(877) 843-7953
website: www.rwjf.org

The Robert Wood Johnson Foundation (RWJF) is the nation's
largest health-focused charity. RWJF works with a variety of
organizations to improve the health and health care of all
Americans. The foundation seeks to identify solutions and
achieve comprehensive, measurable, and timely change. RWJF's
website features many blog posts and articles that have been

published in peer-reviewed journals. Its "Building a Culture of Health" discusses how getting healthy and staying healthy should be top priorities for all Americans.

Shape Up America!
PO Box 149, Clyde Park, MT   59018
website: www.shapeup.org

Shape Up America! is a not-for-profit organization dedicated to raising awareness of the problem of obesity. The organization encourages increased physical activity and healthy eating for all Americans. The Shape Up America! website offers information on healthy weight management and provides health professionals with resources to assist their patients with attaining and maintaining a healthy weight. Its website also provides a variety of other resources, including healthy recipes, a physical activity calculator, and several publications.

World Obesity Federation
Charles Darwin House, 12 Roger Street, London   WCIN 2JU
   United Kingdom
+44 20 7685 2580 • fax: +44 20 7685 2581
e-mail: enquiries@worldobesity.org
website: www.worldobesity.org

The World Obesity Federation (formerly the International Association for the Study of Obesity) is a London-based organization committed to treating, reducing, and preventing obesity globally. The federation creates a global community of organizations by representing professional members of the scientific, medical, and research communities from more than fifty regional and national obesity associations. The federation's website offers subscriptions to its four official journals: *Clinical Obesity, Obesity Reviews, Pediatric Obesity*, and the *International Journal of Obesity*.

Yale Rudd Center for Food Policy & Obesity
Yale University, PO Box 208369, New Haven, CT   06520-8369
(203) 432-6700 • fax: (203) 432-9674

e-mail: rudd.center@yale.edu
website: www.yaleruddcenter.org

The Yale Rudd Center for Food Policy & Obesity is a non-profit research and public policy organization devoted to improving the world's diet, preventing obesity, and reducing weight stigma. The center serves as a leading research institution and clearinghouse for resources that add to the understanding of the complex forces affecting how we eat, how we stigmatize overweight and obese people, and how we can change. On its website, the center offers many publications, including "Putting People First in Obesity" and "Optimal Defaults in the Prevention of Pediatric Obesity: From Platform to Practice."

Bibliography of Books

Linda Bacon

Health at Every Size: The Surprising Truth About Your Weight. Dallas, TX: BenBella, 2010.

Charlotte Biltekoff

Eating Right in America: The Cultural Politics of Food and Health. Durham, NC: Duke University Press, 2013.

Natalie Boero

Killer Fat: Media, Medicine, and Morals in the American "Obesity Epidemic." New Brunswick, NJ: Rutgers University Press, 2012.

W.A. Bogart

Regulating Obesity?: Government, Society, and Questions of Health. New York: Oxford University Press, 2013.

Deborah A. Cohen

A Big Fat Crisis: The Hidden Forces Behind the Obesity Epidemic—and How We Can End It. New York: Nation Books, 2013.

Laura Dawes

Childhood Obesity in America: Biography of an Epidemic. Cambridge, MA: Harvard University Press, 2014.

Amy Erdman Farrell

Fat Shame: Stigma and the Fat Body in American Culture. New York: NYU Press, 2011.

Eric A. Finkelstein and Laurie Zuckerman

The Fattening of America: How the Economy Makes Us Fat, If It Matters, and What to Do About It. New York: Wiley, 2008.

Clare Fleishman

Globesity: 10 Things You Didn't Know Were Making You Fat. Springville, UT: Cedar Fort, 2013.

Michael Gard

The End of the Obesity Epidemic. New Brunswick, NJ: Routledge, 2010.

Julie Guthman

Weighing In: Obesity, Food Justice, and the Limits of Capitalism. Berkeley: University of California Press, 2011.

David W. Haslam, Arya M. Sharma, and Carel W. le Roux, eds.

Controversies in Obesity. New York: Springer, 2014.

April Michelle Herndon

Fat Blame: How the War on Obesity Victimizes Women and Children. Lawrence: University Press of Kansas, 2014.

Samantha Kwan and Jennifer Graves

Framing Fat: Competing Constructions in Contemporary Culture. New Brunswick, NJ: Rutgers, 2013.

Carl J. Lavie

The Obesity Paradox: When Thinner Means Sicker and Heavier Means Healthier. New York: Hudson Street Press, 2014.

Robert H. Lustig

Fat Chance: Beating the Odds Against Sugar, Processed Food, Obesity, and Disease. New York: Hudson Street Press, 2012.

Lonie McMichael

Acceptable Prejudice?: Fat, Rhetoric and Social Justice. Nashville, TN: Pearlsong Press, 2013.

| Michael L. Power and Jay Schulkin | *The Evolution of Obesity.* Baltimore, MD: Johns Hopkins University Press, 2009. |

| Esther Rothblum and Sondra Solovay, eds. | *The Fat Studies Reader.* New York: New York University Press, 2009. |

| Abigail C. Saguy | *What's Wrong with Fat?* New York: Oxford University Press, 2013. |

| Neil Seeman and Patrick Luciani | *XXL: Obesity and the Limits of Shame.* Toronto, ON: University of Toronto Press, 2011. |

| Patricia K. Smith | *Obesity Among Poor Americans: Is Public Assistance the Problem?* Nashville, TN: Vanderbilt University Press, 2009. |

| Gary Taubes | *Why We Get Fat: And What to Do About It.* New York: Knopf, 2010. |

| Georges Vigarello | *The Metamorphoses of Fat: A History of Obesity.* Trans. C. Jon Delogu. New York: Columbia University Press, 2013. |

| Kristin Voigt, Stuart G. Nicholls, Garrath Williams | *Childhood Obesity: Ethical and Policy Issues.* New York: Oxford University Press, 2014. |

| Jacob C. Warren and K. Bryant Smalley | *Always the Fat Kid: The Truth About the Enduring Effects of Childhood Obesity.* New York: Palgrave Macmillan, 2013. |

Jan Wright and Valerie Harwood, eds.   *Biopolitics and the 'Obesity Epidemic':* *Governing Bodies.* New York: Routledge, 2009.

Index

A

Absenteeism, 25
Addiction, 169–170
Adenovirus 36, 201
Adiposity
   and BMI, 35, 36, 38–39
   midlife health effects, 34
   as symptom of disease, 85
Advertising
   anti-obesity campaigns, 136
   regulation debate, 124, 125, 127
   responsibility debate, 31–32, 72
   See also Public awareness
Aetna, 24
Airlines, costs, 25, 26, 53, 137–138, 139
Allison, David B., 15, 150, 197, 200
Almeling, Rene, 20
Alzheimer's disease, 111
American Association of Clinical Endocrinologists, 75
American College of Cardiology, 75
American Heart Association, 75
American Medical Association (AMA)
   Journal of the American Medical Association, 42–43
   obesity classified as disease, 14, 64–65, 67, 68, 74–81, 83
   obesity disease classification, and disagreements, 71–73, 82–87, 99, 102–107

obesity disease classification, and practicality, 69, 98, 99–101
   obesity guidelines, 35
American Obesity Association, 44
American Society for Metabolic and Bariatric Surgery, 72
American Society of Bariatric Physicians, 35, 38
Animal feeds, 182, 183, 184
Animal obesity
   increases, 149–150, 188, 195, 197–198
   research, 149–150, 165–166, 179–180, 197–198, 200–201
Anomaly, Jonny, 132, 189–190
Antibiotic resistance, 186
Antibiotics
   effects on humans, 182, 183–186
   use in animals, 182, 183
Anti-smoking campaigns, 26–27
Assumptions
   accepting stress, 174–175
   obesity epidemic, 45–46
   outdated scientific, 141–142, 202
   prejudices against obese, 67, 70, 71, 72, 73, 75–76, 86, 88, 89, 90–92, 94, 96–97, 104, 131, 141–143, 177, 196–197
   weight loss methods, 15, 55–56, 76, 93, 95–96, 196, 198
Atkinson, Richard L., 197
Australia, 105, 122, 124, 125, 127
Avandia (diabetes drug), 190–191

B

C